Textbook Outlines, Highlights, and Practice Quizzes

Introductory Chemistry

by Nivaldo J. Tro, 5th Edition

All "Just the Facts101" Material Written or Prepared by Cram101 Textbook Reviews

---

Title Page

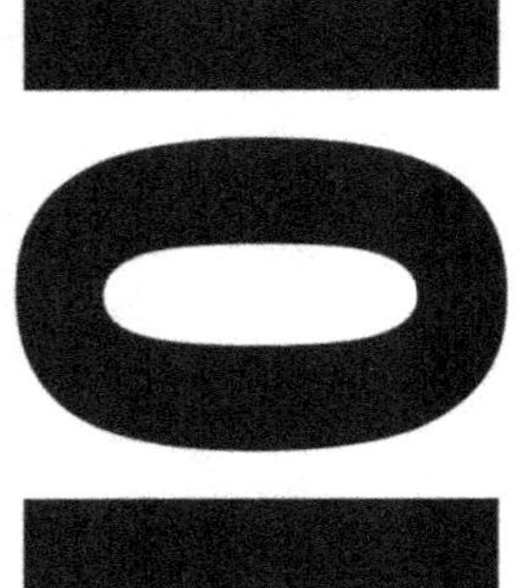

WHY STOP HERE... THERE'S MORE ONLINE

With technology and experience, we've developed tools that make studying easier and efficient. Like this Facts101 textbook notebook, **JustTheFactsl0l.com** offers you the highlights from every chapter of your actual textbook. However, unlike this notebook, **JustTheFactsl0l.com** gives you practice tests for each of the chapters. You also get access to in-depth reference material for writing essays and papers.

JustTheFactsl0l.COM FEATURES:

Outlines & Highlights
Just like the ones in this notebook, but with links to additional information.

Integrated Note Taking
Add your class notes to the Facts101 notes, print them and maximize your study time.

Problem Solving
Step-by-step walk throughs for math, stats and other disciplines.

Practice Exams
Five different test taking formats for every chapter.

Easy Access
Study any of your books, on any computer, anywhere.

Unlimited Textbooks
All the features above for virtually all your textbooks, just add them to your account at no additional cost.

Be sure to use the promo code above when registering on JustTheFactsl0l.com to get 50% off your membership fees.

"Just the Facts101" is a Content Technologies publication and tool designed to give you all the facts from your textbooks. Visit JustTheFacts101.com for the full practice test for each of your chapters for virtually any of your textbooks.

Facts101 has built custom study tools specific to your textbook. We provide all of the factual testable information and unlike traditional study guides, we will never send you back to your textbook for more information.

YOU WILL NEVER HAVE TO HIGHLIGHT A BOOK AGAIN!

Facts101 StudyGuides

All of the information in this StudyGuide is written specifically for your textbook. We include the key terms, places, people, and concepts... the information you can expect on your next exam!

Want to take a practice test?

Throughout each chapter of this StudyGuide you will find links to JustTheFacts101.com where you can select specific chapters to take a complete test on, or you can subscribe and get practice tests for up to 12 of your textbooks, along with other exclusive Jtf101.com tools like problem solving labs and reference libraries.

JustTheFacts101.com

Only Jtf101.com gives you the outlines, highlights, and PRACTICE TESTS specific to your textbook. JustTheFacts101.com is an online application where you'll discover study tools designed to make the most of your limited study time.

By purchasing this book, you get 50% off the normal monthly subscription fee!. Just enter the promotional code **'DK73DW24815'** on the Jtf101.com registration screen.

www.JustTheFacts101.com

ISBN(s): 9781497005228. PUBX-1.201451

Introductory Chemistry
Nivaldo J. Tro, 5th

CONTENTS

1. The Chemical World

CHAPTER OUTLINE: KEY TERMS, PEOPLE, PLACES, CONCEPTS

- Carbon dioxide
- Einstein
- Lewis structure
- Dioxide
- Straw
- Atom
- Molecule
- Carbon
- Nylon
- Atomic theory
- Calx
- Charcoal
- Combustion

1. The Chemical World

CHAPTER HIGHLIGHTS & NOTES: KEY TERMS, PEOPLE, PLACES, CONCEPTS

Carbon dioxide	Carbon dioxide is a naturally occurring chemical compound composed of two oxygen atoms each covalently double bonded to a single carbon atom. It is a gas at standard temperature and pressure and exists in Earth's atmosphere in this state, as a trace gas at a concentration of 0.039 per cent by volume. As part of the carbon cycle, plants, algae, and cyanobacteria use light energy to photosynthesize carbohydrate from carbon dioxide and water, with oxygen produced as a waste product.
Einstein	An einstein is a unit defined as the energy in one mole of photons. Because energy is inversely proportional to wavelength, the unit is frequency dependent. This unit is not part of the International System of Units and is redundant with the joule.
Lewis structure	Lewis structures are diagrams that show the bonding between atoms of a molecule and the lone pairs of electrons that may exist in the molecule. A Lewis structure can be drawn for any covalently bonded molecule, as well as coordination compounds. The Lewis structure was named after Gilbert N
Dioxide	An oxide is a chemical compound that contains at least one oxygen atom and one other element in its chemical formula. Metal oxides typically contain an anion of oxygen in the oxidation state of -2. Most of the Earth's crust consists of solid oxides, the result of elements being oxidized by the oxygen in air or in water. Hydrocarbon combustion affords the two principal carbon oxides: carbon monoxide and carbon dioxide.
Straw	Straw is an agricultural by-product, the dry stalks of cereal plants, after the grain and chaff have been removed. Straw makes up about half of the yield of cereal crops such as barley, oats, rice, rye and wheat. It has many uses, including fuel, livestock bedding and fodder, thatching and basket -making.
Atom	The atom is a basic unit of matter that consists of a dense central nucleus surrounded by a cloud of negatively charged electrons. The atomic nucleus contains a mix of positively charged protons and electrically neutral neutrons, which means 'uncuttable' or 'the smallest indivisible particle of matter'. Although the Indian and Greek concepts of the atom were based purely on philosophy, modern science has retained the name coined by Democritus.
Molecule	A molecule is an electrically neutral group of two or more atoms held together by chemical bonds. Molecules are distinguished from ions by their lack of electrical charge. However, in quantum physics, organic chemistry, and biochemistry, the term molecule is often used less strictly, also being applied to polyatomic ions.
Carbon	Carbon fiber, alternatively graphite fiber, carbon graphite or CF, is a material consisting of fibers about 5-10 μm in diameter and composed mostly of carbon atoms. The carbon atoms are bonded together in crystals that are more or less aligned parallel to the long axis of the fiber.

Nylon	Nylon is a generic designation for a family of synthetic polymers known generically as aliphatic polyamides, first produced on February 28, 1935, by Wallace Carothers at DuPont's research facility at the DuPont Experimental Station. Nylon is one of the most commonly used polymers. Key representatives are nylon-6,6; nylon-6; nylon-6,9; nylon-6,10; nylon-6,12; nylon-11; nylon-12 and nylon-4,6.
Atomic theory	In chemistry and physics, atomic theory is a scientific theory of the nature of matter, which states that matter is composed of discrete units called atoms, as opposed to the earlier concept which held that matter could be divided into any arbitrarily small quantity. It began as a philosophical concept in ancient Greece (Democritus) and entered the scientific mainstream in the early 19th century when discoveries in the field of chemistry showed that matter did indeed behave as if it were made up of particles. The word 'atom' (from the ancient Greek adjective atomos, 'indivisible'.
Calx	Calx is a residual substance, sometimes in the form of a fine powder, that is left when a metal or mineral combusts or is calcinated due to heat. Calx, especially of a metal, is now known as an oxide. According to the obsolete phlogiston theory, the calx was the true elemental substance, having lost its phlogiston in the process of combustion.
Charcoal	Charcoal is a light black residue consisting of carbon, and any remaining ash, obtained by removing water and other volatile constituents from animal and vegetation substances. Charcoal is usually produced by slow pyrolysis, the heating of wood or other substances in the absence of oxygen . It is usually an impure form of carbon as it contains ash; however, sugar charcoal is among the purest forms of carbon readily available, particularly if it is not made by heating but by a dehydration reaction with sulfuric acid to minimise introducing new impurities, as impurities can be removed from the sugar in advance.
Combustion	Combustion or burning is the sequence of exothermic chemical reactions between a fuel and an oxidant accompanied by the production of heat and conversion of chemical species. The release of heat can produce light in the form of either glowing or a flame. In a complete combustion reaction, a compound reacts with an oxidizing element, such as oxygen or fluorine, and the products are compounds of each element in the fuel with the oxidizing element.

1. The Chemical World

CHAPTER QUIZ: KEY TERMS, PEOPLE, PLACES, CONCEPTS

1. _________ is a naturally occurring chemical compound composed of two oxygen atoms each covalently double bonded to a single carbon atom. It is a gas at standard temperature and pressure and exists in Earth's atmosphere in this state, as a trace gas at a concentration of 0.039 per cent by volume.

   As part of the carbon cycle, plants, algae, and cyanobacteria use light energy to photosynthesize carbohydrate from _________ and water, with oxygen produced as a waste product.

   a. Carbon dioxide
   b. Cerium acetylacetonate
   c. Dysprosium acetylacetonate
   d. Gadolinium acetylacetonate

2. An oxide is a chemical compound that contains at least one oxygen atom and one other element in its chemical formula. Metal oxides typically contain an anion of oxygen in the oxidation state of -2. Most of the Earth's crust consists of solid oxides, the result of elements being oxidized by the oxygen in air or in water. Hydrocarbon combustion affords the two principal carbon oxides: carbon monoxide and carbon _________.

   a. Merck Index
   b. covalent
   c. Dioxide
   d. Formal charge

3. An _________ is a unit defined as the energy in one mole of photons. Because energy is inversely proportional to wavelength, the unit is frequency dependent. This unit is not part of the International System of Units and is redundant with the joule.

   a. Einstein
   b. Direct DNA damage
   c. Photochemistry
   d. Daylight

4. _________s are diagrams that show the bonding between atoms of a molecule and the lone pairs of electrons that may exist in the molecule. A _________ can be drawn for any covalently bonded molecule, as well as coordination compounds. The _________ was named after Gilbert N

   a. Bond energy
   b. covalent
   c. Double bond
   d. Lewis structure

5. . _________ is a generic designation for a family of synthetic polymers known generically as aliphatic polyamides, first produced on February 28, 1935, by Wallace Carothers at DuPont's research facility at the DuPont Experimental Station. _________ is one of the most commonly used polymers.

Key representatives are _________-6,6; _________-6; _________-6,9; _________-6,10; _________-6,12; _________-11; _________-12 and _________-4,6.

a. Ban-Lon
b. Basalt fiber
c. Nylon
d. Carbon

ANSWER KEY
1. The Chemical World

---

1. a

2. c

3. a

4. d

5. c

---

2. Measurement and Problem Solving

CHAPTER OUTLINE: KEY TERMS, PEOPLE, PLACES, CONCEPTS

________	Calcium
________	Calcium oxide
________	Algebra
________	Mercury
________	Volume
________	Aspirin
________	Ibuprofen
________	Density
________	Titanium
________	Cholesterol

CHAPTER HIGHLIGHTS & NOTES: KEY TERMS, PEOPLE, PLACES, CONCEPTS

Calcium	Calcium is the chemical element with symbol Ca and atomic number 20. Calcium is a soft gray alkaline earth metal, and is the fifth-most-abundant element by mass in the Earth's crust. Calcium is also the fifth-most-abundant dissolved ion in seawater by both molarity and mass, after sodium, chloride, magnesium, and sulfate. Calcium is essential for living organisms, in particular in cell physiology, where movement of the calcium ion Ca^{2+} into and out of the cytoplasm functions as a signal for many cellular processes.
Calcium oxide	Calcium oxide, commonly known as quicklime or burnt lime, is a widely used chemical compound. It is a white, caustic, alkaline crystalline solid at room temperature. The broadly used term 'lime' connotes calcium-containing inorganic materials, which include carbonates, oxides and hydroxides of calcium, silicon, magnesium, aluminium, and iron predominate, such as limestone.
Algebra	Algebra is one of the broad parts of mathematics, together with number theory, geometry and analysis.

As such, it includes everything from elementary equation solving to the study of abstractions such as groups, rings, and fields. The more basic parts of algebra are called elementary algebra, the more abstract parts are called abstract algebra or modern algebra.

Mercury

Mercury is a chemical element with the symbol Hg and atomic number 80. It is commonly known as quicksilver and was formerly named hydrargyrum (from Greek 'hydr-' water and 'argyros' silver). A heavy, silvery d-block element, mercury is the only metal that is liquid at standard conditions for temperature and pressure; the only other element that is liquid under these conditions is bromine, though metals such as caesium, gallium, and rubidium melt just above room temperature. With a freezing point of -38.83 °C and boiling point of 356.73 °C, mercury has one of the narrowest ranges of its liquid state of any metal.

Volume

In thermodynamics, the volume of a system is an important extensive parameter for describing its thermodynamic state. The specific volume, an intensive property, is the system's volume per unit of mass. Volume is a function of state and is interdependent with other thermodynamic properties such as pressure and temperature.

Aspirin

Aspirin, also known as acetylsalicylic acid (INN (?--?l--i--ik) ASA), is a salicylate drug, often used as an analgesic to relieve minor aches and pains, as an antipyretic to reduce fever, and as an anti-inflammatory medication. Aspirin was first isolated by Felix Hoffmann, a chemist with the German company Bayer in 1897.

Salicylic acid, the main metabolite of aspirin, is an integral part of human and animal metabolism.

Ibuprofen

Ibuprofen is a nonsteroidal anti-inflammatory drug (NSAID) used for pain relief, fever reduction, and for reducing swelling.

Ibuprofen has an antiplatelet effect, though relatively mild and somewhat short-lived compared with aspirin or prescription antiplatelet drugs. In general, ibuprofen also has a vasodilation effect.

Density

The density, or more precisely, the volumetric mass density, of a substance is its mass per unit volume. The symbol most often used for density is ? (the lower case Greek letter rho).

Mathematically, density is defined as mass divided by volume: $\rho = \frac{m}{V},$

where ? is the density, m is the mass, and V is the volume.

Titanium

Titanium is a chemical element with the symbol Ti and atomic number 22. It is a lustrous transition metal with a silver color, low density and high strength. It is highly resistant to corrosion in sea water, aqua regia and chlorine.

2. Measurement and Problem Solving

CHAPTER HIGHLIGHTS & NOTES: KEY TERMS, PEOPLE, PLACES, CONCEPTS

Cholesterol	Cholesterol, from the Ancient Greek chole- and stereos (solid) followed by the chemical suffix -ol for an alcohol, is an organic molecule. It is a sterol (or modified steroid), and an essential structural component of animal cell membranes that is required to establish proper membrane permeability and fluidity. Cholesterol is thus considered within the class of lipid molecules.

CHAPTER QUIZ: KEY TERMS, PEOPLE, PLACES, CONCEPTS

1. _________ is a chemical element with the symbol Hg and atomic number 80. It is commonly known as quicksilver and was formerly named hydrargyrum (from Greek 'hydr-' water and 'argyros' silver). A heavy, silvery d-block element, _________ is the only metal that is liquid at standard conditions for temperature and pressure; the only other element that is liquid under these conditions is bromine, though metals such as caesium, gallium, and rubidium melt just above room temperature. With a freezing point of -38.83 °C and boiling point of 356.73 °C, _________ has one of the narrowest ranges of its liquid state of any metal.

   a. Barium
   b. Mercury
   c. Beryllium
   d. Bismuth

2. _________ is one of the broad parts of mathematics, together with number theory, geometry and analysis. As such, it includes everything from elementary equation solving to the study of abstractions such as groups rings, and fields. The more basic parts of _________ are called elementary _________, the more abstract parts are called abstract _________ or modern _________.

   a. Algebra
   b. Boron trioxide
   c. Barium acetylacetonate
   d. Cerium acetylacetonate

3. . _________ is the chemical element with symbol Ca and atomic number 20. _________ is a soft gray alkaline earth metal, and is the fifth-most-abundant element by mass in the Earth's crust. _________ is also the fifth-most-abundant dissolved ion in seawater by both molarity and mass, after sodium, chloride, magnesium, and sulfate.

   _________ is essential for living organisms, in particular in cell physiology, where movement of the _________ ion Ca^{2+} into and out of the cytoplasm functions as a signal for many cellular processes.

   a. Barium
   b. Berkelium

c. Beryllium
d. Calcium

4. _________, commonly known as quicklime or burnt lime, is a widely used chemical compound. It is a white, caustic, alkaline crystalline solid at room temperature. The broadly used term 'lime' connotes calcium-containing inorganic materials, which include carbonates, oxides and hydroxides of calcium, silicon, magnesium, aluminium, and iron predominate, such as limestone.

   a. Barium oxide
   b. Boron trioxide
   c. Barium acetylacetonate
   d. Calcium oxide

5. In thermodynamics, the _________ of a system is an important extensive parameter for describing its thermodynamic state. The specific _________, an intensive property, is the system's _________ per unit of mass. _________ is a function of state and is interdependent with other thermodynamic properties such as pressure and temperature.

   a. Volume
   b. Bjerrum length
   c. Boiling-point elevation
   d. Bolaamphiphile

ANSWER KEY
2. Measurement and Problem Solving

---

1. b
2. a
3. d
4. d
5. a

---

3. Matter and Energy

CHAPTER OUTLINE: KEY TERMS, PEOPLE, PLACES, CONCEPTS

- Graphite
- Lewis structure
- Bohr model
- Isopropyl alcohol
- Molecule
- Atom
- Radiation
- Amorphous solid
- Quartz
- Sodium oxide
- States of matter
- Carbon dioxide
- Compressibility
- Helium
- Mendelevium
- Miscibility
- Oxygen
- Glycolipid
- Phospholipid
- Steroid
- Carbon

3. Matter and Energy

CHAPTER OUTLINE: KEY TERMS, PEOPLE, PLACES, CONCEPTS

- Brass
- Nitrite
- Decomposition
- Homogeneous
- Physical properties
- Evaporation
- Product
- Distillation
- Filtration
- Butane
- Kinetic energy
- Potential energy
- Thermal energy
- Forms of energy
- Calorie
- Chemical energy
- Excited state
- Trinitrotoluene
- Celsius
- Fahrenheit
- Fructose

3. Matter and Energy

CHAPTER OUTLINE: KEY TERMS, PEOPLE, PLACES, CONCEPTS

	Electron
	Neutron
	Proton
	Heat capacity
	Calcium oxide
	Ibuprofen

CHAPTER HIGHLIGHTS & NOTES: KEY TERMS, PEOPLE, PLACES, CONCEPTS

Graphite

The mineral graphite is an allotrope of carbon. It was named by Abraham Gottlcb Werner in 1789 from the Ancient Greek ???f? (grapho), 'to draw/write', for its use in pencils, where it is commonly called lead (not to be confused with the metallic element lead). Unlike diamond (another carbon allotrope), graphite is an electrical conductor, a semimetal.

Lewis structure

Lewis structures are diagrams that show the bonding between atoms of a molecule and the lone pairs of electrons that may exist in the molecule. A Lewis structure can be drawn for any covalently bonded molecule, as well as coordination compounds. The Lewis structure was named after Gilbert N

Bohr model

In atomic physics, the Bohr model, introduced by Niels Bohr in 1913, depicts the atom as small, positively charged nucleus surrounded by electrons that travel in circular orbits around the nucleus--similar in structure to the solar system, but with attraction provided by electrostatic forces rather than gravity. After the cubic model .•Quantum ruleThe angular momentum L = $m_e vr$ is an integer multiple of h: $m_e vr = n\hbar$ Substituting the expression for the velocity gives an equation for r in terms of n: $\sqrt{Zk_e e^2 m_e r} = n\hbar$ so that the allowed orbit radius at any n is: $r_n = \frac{n^2\hbar^2}{Zk_e e^2 m_e}$ The smallest possible value of r in the hydrogen atom is called the Bohr radius and is equal to:

$$r_1 = \frac{\hbar^2}{k_e e^2 m_e} \approx 5.29 \times 10^{-11}\mathrm{m}$$

The energy of the n-th level for any atom is determined by the radius and quantum number:

$$E = -\frac{Z k_e e^2}{2 r_n} = -\frac{Z^2 (k_e e^2)^2 m_e}{2\hbar^2 n^2} \approx \frac{-13.6 Z^2}{n^2}\mathrm{eV}$$

An electron in the lowest energy level of hydrogen therefore has about 13.6 eV less energy than a motionless electron infinitely far from the nucleus. The next energy level is -3.4 eV. The third (n = 3) is -1.51 eV, and so on.

Isopropyl alcohol

Isopropyl alcohol is a common name for a chemical compound with the molecular formula C_3H_8O or C_3H_7OH. It is a colorless, flammable chemical compound with a strong odor. It is the simplest example of a secondary alcohol, where the alcohol carbon atom is attached to two other carbon atoms sometimes shown as $(CH_3)_2CHOH$. It is a structural isomer of propanol. Isopropyl alcohol is denatured for certain uses, in which case the NFPA 704 rating is changed to 2,3,1.

Molecule

A molecule is an electrically neutral group of two or more atoms held together by chemical bonds. Molecules are distinguished from ions by their lack of electrical charge. However, in quantum physics, organic chemistry, and biochemistry, the term molecule is often used less strictly, also being applied to polyatomic ions.

Atom

The atom is a basic unit of matter that consists of a dense central nucleus surrounded by a cloud of negatively charged electrons. The atomic nucleus contains a mix of positively charged protons and electrically neutral neutrons, which means 'uncuttable' or 'the smallest indivisible particle of matter'. Although the Indian and Greek concepts of the atom were based purely on philosophy, modern science has retained the name coined by Democritus.

Radiation

In physics, radiation is a process in which energetic particles or energetic waves travel through a vacuum, or through matter-containing media that are not required for their propagation. Waves of a mass filled medium itself, such as water waves or sound waves, are usually not considered to be forms of 'radiation' in this sense.

Radiation can be classified as either ionizing or non-ionizing according to whether it ionizes or does not ionize ordinary chemical matter.

Amorphous solid

In condensed matter physics, an amorphous or non-crystalline solid is a solid that lacks the long-range order characteristic of a crystal.

In some older books, the term has been used synonymously with glass.

Quartz

Quartz is the second most abundant mineral in the Earth's continental crust, after feldspar. It is made up of a continuous framework of SiO_4 silicon-oxygen tetrahedra, with each oxygen being shared between two tetrahedra, giving an overall formula SiO_2.

There are many different varieties of quartz, several of which are semi-precious gemstones.

Sodium oxide

Sodium oxide is a chemical compound with the formula Na_2O. It is used in ceramics and glasses, though not in a raw form. Treatment with water affords sodium hydroxide. Na_2O + H_2O ? 2 NaOH

The alkali metal oxides M_2O (M = Li, Na, K, Rb) crystallise in the antifluorite structure.

States of matter

In physics, a state of matter is one of the distinct forms that different phases of matter take on. Four states of matter are observable in everyday life: solid, liquid, gas, and plasma. Many other states are known such as Bose-Einstein condensates and neutron-degenerate matter but these only occur in extreme situations such as ultra cold or ultra dense matter.

Carbon dioxide

Carbon dioxide is a naturally occurring chemical compound composed of two oxygen atoms each covalently double bonded to a single carbon atom. It is a gas at standard temperature and pressure and exists in Earth's atmosphere in this state, as a trace gas at a concentration of 0.039 per cent by volume.

As part of the carbon cycle, plants, algae, and cyanobacteria use light energy to photosynthesize carbohydrate from carbon dioxide and water, with oxygen produced as a waste product.

Compressibility

In thermodynamics and fluid mechanics, compressibility is a measure of the relative volume change of a fluid or solid as a response to a pressure change.

$$\beta = -\frac{1}{V}\frac{\partial V}{\partial p}$$

where V is volume and p is pressure.

Helium

Helium is a chemical element with symbol He and atomic number 2. It is a colorless, odorless, tasteless, non-toxic, inert, monatomic gas that heads the noble gas group in the periodic table. Its boiling and melting points are the lowest among the elements and it exists only as a gas except in extreme conditions.

Helium is the second lightest element and is the second most abundant element in the observable universe, being present at about 24% of the total elemental mass, which is more than 12 times the mass of all the heavier elements combined.

Mendelevium

Mendelevium is a synthetic element with the symbol Md and the atomic number 101.

A metallic radioactive transuranic element in the actinide series, mendelevium is usually synthesized by bombarding einsteinium with alpha particles. It was named after Dmitri Ivanovich Mendeleev, who created the periodic table, the standard way to classify all the chemical elements.

Miscibility

Miscibility is the property of substances to mix in all proportions, forming a homogeneous solution. The term is most often used to refer to liquids, but applies also to solids and gases. Water and ethanol, for example, are miscible because they mix in all proportions.

Oxygen

Oxygen is a chemical element with symbol O and atomic number 8. It is a member of the chalcogen group on the periodic table and is a highly reactive nonmetallic element and oxidizing agent that readily forms compounds (notably oxides) with most elements. By mass, oxygen is the third-most abundant element in the universe, after hydrogen and helium At STP, two atoms of the element bind to form dioxygen, a diatomic gas that is colorless, odorless, and tasteless; with the formula O2.

Many major classes of organic molecules in living organisms, such as proteins, nucleic acids, carbohydrates, and fats, contain oxygen, as do the major inorganic compounds that are constituents of animal shells, teeth, and bone.

Glycolipid

Glycolipids are lipids with a carbohydrate attached. Their role is to provide energy and also serve as markers for cellular recognition.

Phospholipid

Phospholipids are a class of lipids that are a major component of all cell membranes as they can form lipid bilayers. Most phospholipids contain a diglyceride, a phosphate group, and a simple organic molecule such as choline; one exception to this rule is sphingomyelin, which is derived from sphingosine instead of glycerol. The first phospholipid identified as such in biological tissues was lecithin, or phosphatidylcholine, in the egg yolk, by Theodore Nicolas Gobley, a French chemist and pharmacist, in 1847. The structure of the phospholipid molecule generally consists of hydrophobic tails and a hydrophilic head.

Steroid

A steroid is a type of organic compound that contains a characteristic arrangement of four cycloalkane rings that are joined to each other. Examples of steroids include the dietary fat cholesterol, the sex hormones estradiol and testosterone and the anti-inflammatory drug dexamethasone.

The core of steroids is composed of twenty carbon atoms bonded together that take the form of four fused rings: three cyclohexane rings (designated as rings A, B and C in the figure to the right) and one cyclopentane ring (the D ring).

Carbon

Carbon fiber, alternatively graphite fiber, carbon graphite or CF, is a material consisting of fibers about 5-10 μm in diameter and composed mostly of carbon atoms. The carbon atoms are bonded together in crystals that are more or less aligned parallel to the long axis of the fiber.

Brass	Brass is an alloy made of copper and zinc; the proportions of zinc and copper can be varied to create a range of brasses with varying properties. By comparison, bronze is principally an alloy of copper and tin. Bronze does not necessarily contain tin, and a variety of alloys of copper, including alloys with arsenic, phosphorus, aluminium, manganese, and silicon, are commonly termed 'bronze'.
Nitrite	The nitrite ion, which has the chemical formula NO_2^-, is a symmetric anion with equal N-O bond lengths and an O-N-O bond angle of approximately 120°. Upon protonation, the unstable weak acid nitrous acid is produced. Nitrite can be oxidized or reduced, with the product somewhat dependent on the oxidizing/reducing agent and its strength.
Decomposition	Decomposition is the process by which organic substances are broken down into simpler forms of matter. The process is essential for recycling the finite matter that occupies physical space in the biome. Bodies of living organisms begin to decompose shortly after death.
Homogeneous	Homogeneous as a term in physical chemistry and material science refers to substances and mixtures which are in a single phase. This is in contrast to a substance that is heterogeneous. The definition of homogeneous strongly depends on the context used.
Physical properties	A physical property is any property that is measurable whose value describes a state of a physical system. The changes in the physical properties of a system can be used to describe its transformations or evolutions between its momentary states. Physical properties are often referred to as observables.
Evaporation	Evaporation is a type of vaporization of a liquid that occurs from the surface of a liquid into a gaseous phase that is not saturated with the evaporating substance. The other type of vaporization is boiling, which, instead, occurs within the entire mass of the liquid and can also take place when the vapor phase is saturated, such as when steam is produced in a boiler. Evaporation that occurs directly from the solid phase below the melting point, as commonly observed with ice at or below freezing or moth crystals (napthalene or paradichlorobenzine), is called sublimation.
Product	Product are formed during chemical reactions as reagents are consumed. Products have lower energy than the reagents and are produced during the reaction according to the second law of thermodynamics. The released energy comes from changes in chemical bonds between atoms in reagent molecules and may be given off in the form of heat or light.
Distillation	Distillation is a method of separating mixtures based on differences in volatility of components in a boiling liquid mixture. Distillation is a unit operation, or a physical separation process, and not a chemical reaction.

3. Matter and Energy

CHAPTER HIGHLIGHTS & NOTES: KEY TERMS, PEOPLE, PLACES, CONCEPTS

Filtration	Filtration is commonly the mechanical or physical operation which is used for the separation of solids from fluids by interposing a medium through which only the fluid can pass. The fluid that pass through is called a filtrate. Oversize solids in the fluid are retained, but the separation is not complete; solids will be contaminated with some fluid and filtrate will contain fine particles (depending on the pore size and filter thickness).
Butane	Butane is an organic compound with the formula C_4H_{10} that is an alkane with four carbon atoms. Butane is a gas at room temperature and atmospheric pressure. The term may refer to either of two structural isomers, n-butane or isobutane or to a mixture of these isomers.
Kinetic energy	In physics, the kinetic energy of an object is the energy which it possesses due to its motion. It is defined as the work needed to accelerate a body of a given mass from rest to its stated velocity. Having gained this energy during its acceleration, the body maintains this kinetic energy unless its speed changes.
Potential energy	In physics, potential energy is energy stored in a system of forcefully interacting physical entities. The SI unit for measuring work and energy is the joule (symbol J). The term potential energy was introduced by the 19th century Scottish engineer and physicist William Rankine, although it has links to Greek philosopher Aristotle's concept of potentiality.
Thermal energy	Thermal energy is the part of the total potential energy and kinetic energy of an object or sample of matter that results in the system temperature. It is represented by the variable Q, and can be measured in Joules. This quantity may be difficult to determine or even meaningless unless the system has attained its temperature only through warming (heating), and not been subjected to work input or output, or any other energy-changing processes.
Forms of energy	In the context of physical sciences, several forms of energy have been identified. These include:•Heat is just that amount of thermal energy being transferred (in a given process) in the direction of decreasing temperature.•Mechanical work is just that amount of (mechanical) energy being transferred (in a given process) due to displacement in the direction of an applied force. Some entries in the above list constitute or comprise others in the list. The list is not necessarily complete.
Calorie	The name calorie is used for two units of energy. •The small calorie or gram calorie is the approximate amount of energy needed to raise the temperature of one gram of water by one degree Celsius.•The large calorie, kilogram calorie, dietary calorie, nutritionist's calorie or food calorie is the amount of energy needed to raise the temperature of one kilogram of water by one degree Celsius. The large calorie is thus equal to 1000 small calories or one kilocalorie.

Chemical energy

In chemistry, Chemical energy is the potential of a chemical substance to undergo a transformation through a chemical reaction or, to transform other chemical substances. Examples include batteries and light bulbs and cells etc. Breaking or making of chemical bonds involves energy, which may be either absorbed or evolved from a chemical system.

Excited state

Excitation is an elevation in energy level above an arbitrary baseline energy state. In physics there is a specific technical definition for energy level which is often associated with an atom being excited to an excited state.

In quantum mechanics an excited state of a system (such as an atom, molecule or nucleus) is any quantum state of the system that has a higher energy than the ground state (that is, more energy than the absolute minimum).

Trinitrotoluene

Trinitrotoluene, or more specifically, 2,4,6-trinitrotoluene, is a chemical compound with the formula $C_6H_2(NO_2)_3CH_3$. This yellow-colored solid is sometimes used as a reagent in chemical synthesis, but it is best known as a useful explosive material with convenient handling properties. The explosive yield of TNT is considered to be the standard measure of strength of bombs and other explosives.

Celsius

Celsius, also known as centigrade, is a scale and unit of measurement for temperature. It is named after the Swedish astronomer Anders Celsius who developed a similar temperature scale. The degree Celsius can refer to a specific temperature on the Celsius scale as well as a unit to indicate a temperature interval, a difference between two temperatures or an uncertainty.

Fahrenheit

Fahrenheit is a temperature scale based on one proposed in 1724 by the physicist Daniel Gabriel Fahrenheit after whom the scale is named. The scale is defined by two fixed points: the temperature at which water freezes into ice is defined as 32 degrees, and the boiling point of water is defined to be 212 degrees. On Fahrenheit's original scale the lower defining point was the freezing point of brine, defined as zero degrees.

Fructose

Fructose, or fruit sugar, is a simple monosaccharide found in many plants, where it is often bonded to glucose to form the disaccharide sucrose. It is one of the three dietary monosaccharides, along with glucose and galactose, that are absorbed directly into the bloodstream during digestion. Fructose was discovered by French chemist Augustin-Pierre Dubrunfaut in 1847. Pure, dry fructose is a very sweet, white, odorless, crystalline solid and is the most water-soluble of all the sugars.

Electron

The electron is a subatomic particle with a negative elementary electric charge Electrons belong to the first generation of the lepton particle family, and are generally thought to be elementary particles because they have no known components or substructure. The electron has a mass that is approximately 1/1836 that of the proton.

Neutron

The neutron is a subatomic hadron particle that has the symbol n or n

	0, no net electric charge and a mass slightly larger than that of a proton. With the exception of hydrogen-1, nuclei of atoms consist of protons and neutrons, which are therefore collectively referred to as nucleons. The number of protons in a nucleus is the atomic number and defines the type of element the atom forms.
Proton	The proton is a subatomic particle with the symbol p or p+ and a positive electric charge of 1 elementary charge. One or more protons are present in the nucleus of each atom. The number of protons in each atom is its atomic number.
Heat capacity	Heat capacity, or thermal capacity, is the measurable physical quantity of heat energy required to change the temperature of an object or body by a given amount. The SI unit of heat capacity is joule per kelvin, $\frac{J}{K}$ and the dimensional form is $M^1L^2T^{-2}T^{-1}$. Heat capacity is an extensive property of matter, meaning it is proportional to the size of the system.
Calcium oxide	Calcium oxide, commonly known as quicklime or burnt lime, is a widely used chemical compound. It is a white, caustic, alkaline crystalline solid at room temperature. The broadly used term 'lime' connotes calcium-containing inorganic materials, which include carbonates, oxides and hydroxides of calcium, silicon, magnesium, aluminium, and iron predominate, such as limestone.
Ibuprofen	Ibuprofen is a nonsteroidal anti-inflammatory drug (NSAID) used for pain relief, fever reduction, and for reducing swelling. Ibuprofen has an antiplatelet effect, though relatively mild and somewhat short-lived compared with aspirin or prescription antiplatelet drugs. In general, ibuprofen also has a vasodilation effect.

1. _________ is a synthetic element with the symbol Md and the atomic number 101. A metallic radioactive transuranic element in the actinide series, _________ is usually synthesized by bombarding einsteinium with alpha particles. It was named after Dmitri Ivanovich Mendeleev, who created the periodic table, the standard way to classify all the chemical elements.

   a. Barium
   b. Berkelium
   c. Mendelevium
   d. Bismuth

2. _________ is a temperature scale based on one proposed in 1724 by the physicist Daniel Gabriel _________ after whom the scale is named. The scale is defined by two fixed points: the temperature at which water freezes into ice is defined as 32 degrees, and the boiling point of water is defined to be 212 degrees. On _________'s original scale the lower defining point was the freezing point of brine, defined as zero degrees.

   a. Fahrenheit
   b. Degree of frost
   c. Delisle scale
   d. CrystaSulf

3. _________ is the process by which organic substances are broken down into simpler forms of matter. The process is essential for recycling the finite matter that occupies physical space in the biome. Bodies of living organisms begin to decompose shortly after death.

   a. Biochemical oxygen demand
   b. Decomposition
   c. Biofuel
   d. Biogas upgrader

4. The mineral _________ is an allotrope of carbon. It was named by Abraham Gottlob Werner in 1789 from the Ancient Greek ???f? (grapho), 'to draw/write', for its use in pencils, where it is commonly called lead (not to be confused with the metallic element lead). Unlike diamond (another carbon allotrope), _________ is an electrical conductor, a semimetal.

   a. Bamboo charcoal
   b. Benzotriyne
   c. Graphite
   d. Carbide-derived carbon

5. . _________s are lipids with a carbohydrate attached. Their role is to provide energy and also serve as markers for cellular recognition.

   a. Glycolipid
   b. Carbohydrate chemistry
   c. Carbohydrate conformation

ANSWER KEY
3. Matter and Energy

---

1. c
2. a
3. b
4. c
5. a

---

4. Atoms and Elements

CHAPTER OUTLINE: KEY TERMS, PEOPLE, PLACES, CONCEPTS

- Amine
- Lewis structure
- Silicate
- Silicon
- Triethylamine
- Atomic theory
- Scanning tunneling microscope
- Electron
- Neutron
- Proton
- Bohr model
- Carbon
- Rutherford
- Thomson
- Atomic mass
- Atomic mass unit
- Atom
- Helium
- Uranium
- Radiation
- Argon

4. Atoms and Elements

CHAPTER OUTLINE: KEY TERMS, PEOPLE, PLACES, CONCEPTS

______ Atomic number

______ Bromine

______ Periodic table

______ Potassium

______ Straw

______ Americium

______ Curie

______ Curium

______ Francium

______ Mendelevium

______ Polonium

______ Chromium

______ Germanium

______ Metalloid

______ Nonmetal

______ Arsenic

______ Semiconductor

______ Algebra

______ Alkali metal

______ Alkaline earth metal

______ Barium

4. Atoms and Elements

CHAPTER OUTLINE: KEY TERMS, PEOPLE, PLACES, CONCEPTS

________	Calcium
________	Fluorine
________	Ground state
________	Halogen
________	Krypton
________	Lithium
________	Rubidium
________	Strontium
________	Xenon
________	Alkali
________	Chloride ion
________	Sodium
________	Sodium chloride
________	Valence electron
________	Beryllium
________	Chloride
________	Isotope
________	Mass number

4. Atoms and Elements

CHAPTER HIGHLIGHTS & NOTES: KEY TERMS, PEOPLE, PLACES, CONCEPTS

Amine	Amines are organic compounds and functional groups that contain a basic nitrogen atom with a lone pair. Amines are derivatives of ammonia, wherein one or more hydrogen atoms have been replaced by a substituent such as an alkyl or aryl group. Important amines include amino acids, biogenic amines, trimethylamine, and aniline; see Category:Amines for a list of amines.
Lewis structure	Lewis structures are diagrams that show the bonding between atoms of a molecule and the lone pairs of electrons that may exist in the molecule. A Lewis structure can be drawn for any covalently bonded molecule, as well as coordination compounds. The Lewis structure was named after Gilbert N
Silicate	Silicate compounds, including the minerals, consist of silicate anions whose charge is balanced by various cations. Myriad silicate anions can exist, and each can form compounds with many different cations. Hence this class of compounds is very large.
Silicon	Silicon, a tetravalent metalloid, is a chemical element with the symbol Si and atomic number 14. It is less reactive than its chemical analog carbon, the nonmetal directly above it in the periodic table, but more reactive than germanium, the metalloid directly below it in the table. Controversy about silicon's character dates to its discovery; it was first prepared and characterized in pure form in 1823. In 1808, it was given the name silicium (from Latin: silex, hard stone or flint), with an -ium word-ending to suggest a metal, a name which the element retains in several non-English languages. However, its final English name, first suggested in 1817, reflects the more physically similar elements carbon and boron.
Triethylamine	Triethylamine is the chemical compound with the formula N_3, commonly abbreviated Et_3N. It is also abbreviated TEA, yet this abbreviation must be used carefully to avoid confusion with triethanolamine or tetraethylammonium, for which TEA is also a common abbreviation. It is a colourless volatile liquid with a strong fishy odor reminiscent of ammonia and is also the smell of the hawthorn plant. Like diisopropylethylamine (Hünig's base), triethylamine is commonly encountered in organic synthesis.
Atomic theory	In chemistry and physics, atomic theory is a scientific theory of the nature of matter, which states that matter is composed of discrete units called atoms, as opposed to the earlier concept which held that matter could be divided into any arbitrarily small quantity. It began as a philosophical concept in ancient Greece (Democritus) and entered the scientific mainstream in the early 19th century when discoveries in the field of chemistry showed that matter did indeed behave as if it were made up of particles. The word 'atom' (from the ancient Greek adjective atomos, 'indivisible'.
Scanning tunneling microscope	A scanning tunneling microscope is an instrument for imaging surfaces at the atomic level. Its development in 1981 earned its inventors, Gerd Binnig and Heinrich Rohrer (at IBM Zürich), the Nobel Prize in Physics in 1986.

For an Scanning tunneling microscope, good resolution is considered to be 0.· nm lateral resolution and 0.01 nm depth resolution. With this resolution, individual atoms within materials are routinely imaged and manipulated.

Electron

The electron is a subatomic particle with a negative elementary electric charge. Electrons belong to the first generation of the lepton particle family, and are generally thought to be elementary particles because they have no known components or substructure. The electron has a mass that is approximately 1/1836 that of the proton.

Neutron

The neutron is a subatomic hadron particle that has the symbol n or n0, no net electric charge and a mass slightly larger than that of a proton. With the exception of hydrogen-1, nuclei of atoms consist of protons and neutrons, which are therefore collectively referred to as nucleons. The number of protons in a nucleus is the atomic number and defines the type of element the atom forms.

Proton

The proton is a subatomic particle with the symbol p or p+ and a positive electric charge of 1 elementary charge. One or more protons are present in the nucleus of each atom. The number of protons in each atom is its atomic number.

Bohr model

In atomic physics, the Bohr model, introduced by Niels Bohr in 1913, depicts the atom as small, positively charged nucleus surrounded by electrons that travel in circular orbits around the nucleus--similar in structure to the solar system, but with attraction provided by electrostatic forces rather than gravity. After the cubic model .•Quantum ruleThe angular momentum L = $m_e vr$ is an integer multiple of h: $m_e vr = n\hbar$ Substituting the expression for the velocity gives an equation for r in terms of n: $\sqrt{Zk_e e^2 m_e r} = n\hbar$ so that the allowed orbit radius at any n is: $r_n = \frac{n^2\hbar^2}{Zk_e e^2 m_e}$ The smallest possible value of r in the hydrogen atom is called the Bohr radius and is equal to: $r_1 = \frac{\hbar^2}{k_e e^2 m_e} \approx 5.29 \times 10^{-11}\mathrm{m}$ The energy of the n-th level for any atom is determined by the radius and quantum number:

$$E = -\frac{Zk_e e^2}{2r_n} = -\frac{Z^2(k_e e^2)^2 m_e}{2\hbar^2 n^2} \approx \frac{-13.6Z^2}{n^2}\mathrm{eV}$$

An electron in the lowest energy level of hydrogen therefore has about 13.6 eV less energy than a motionless electron infinitely far from the nucleus. The next energy level is -3.4 eV. The third (n = 3) is -1.51 eV, and so on.

Carbon

Carbon fiber, alternatively graphite fiber, carbon graphite or CF, is a material consisting of fibers about 5-10 μm in diameter and composed mostly of carbon atoms.

The carbon atoms are bonded together in crystals that are more or less aligned parallel to the long axis of the fiber. The crystal alignment gives the fiber high strength-to-volume ratio (making it strong for its size).

Rutherford

The rutherford is an obsolete unit of radioactivity, defined as the activity of a quantity of radioactive material in which one million nuclei decay per second. It is therefore equivalent to one megabecquerel. It was named after Ernest Rutherford.

Thomson

The thomson is a unit that has appeared infrequently in scientific literature relating to the field of mass spectrometry as a unit of mass-to-charge ratio. The unit was proposed by Cooks and Rockwood naming it in honour of J. J. Thomson who measured the mass-to-charge ratio of electrons and ions.

Atomic mass

The atomic mass is the mass of an atomic particle, sub-atomic particle, or molecule. It may be expressed in unified atomic mass units; by international agreement, 1 atomic mass unit is defined as 1/12 of the mass of a single carbon-12 atom (at rest). When expressed in such units, the atomic mass is called the relative isotopic mass .

Atomic mass unit

The unified atomic mass unit or dalton (symbol: Da) is the standard unit that is used for indicating mass on an atomic or molecular scale (atomic mass). One unified atomic mass unit is approximately the mass of a nucleon and is equivalent to 1 g/mol. It is defined as one twelfth of the mass of an unbound neutral atom of carbon-12 in its nuclear and electronic ground state, and has a value of $1.660538921(73)\times10^{-27}$ kg.

Atom

The atom is a basic unit of matter that consists of a dense central nucleus surrounded by a cloud of negatively charged electrons. The atomic nucleus contains a mix of positively charged protons and electrically neutral neutrons, which means 'uncuttable' or 'the smallest indivisible particle of matter'. Although the Indian and Greek concepts of the atom were based purely on philosophy, modern science has retained the name coined by Democritus.

Helium

Helium is a chemical element with symbol He and atomic number 2. It is a colorless, odorless, tasteless, non-toxic, inert, monatomic gas that heads the noble gas group in the periodic table. Its boiling and melting points are the lowest among the elements and it exists only as a gas except in extreme conditions.

Helium is the second lightest element and is the second most abundant element in the observable universe, being present at about 24% of the total elemental mass, which is more than 12 times the mass of all the heavier elements combined.

Uranium

Uranium is a silvery-white metallic chemical element in the actinide series of the periodic table, with symbol U and atomic number 92. A uranium atom has 92 protons and 92 electrons, of which 6 are valence electrons. Uranium is weakly radioactive because all its isotopes are unstable.

4. Atoms and Elements

Radiation

In physics, radiation is a process in which energetic particles or energetic waves travel through a vacuum, or through matter-containing media that are not required for their propagation. Waves of a mass filled medium itself, such as water waves or sound waves, are usually not considered to be forms of 'radiation' in this sense.

Radiation can be classified as either ionizing or non-ionizing according to whether it ionizes or does not ionize ordinary chemical matter.

Argon

Argon is a chemical element with symbol Ar and atomic number 18. It is in group 18 of the periodic table and is a noble gas. Argon is the third most common gas in the Earth's atmosphere, at 0.93% (9,300 ppm), making it approximately 23.8 times as abundant as the next most common atmospheric gas, carbon dioxide (390 ppm), and more than 500 times as abundant as the next most common noble gas, neon (18 ppm). Nearly all of this argon is radiogenic argon-40 derived from the decay of potassium-40 in the Earth's crust.

Atomic number

In chemistry and physics, the atomic number is the number of protons found in the nucleus of an atom and therefore identical to the charge number of the nucleus. It is conventionally represented by the symbol Z. The atomic number uniquely identifies a chemical element. In an atom of neutral charge, the atomic number is also equal to the number of electrons.

Bromine

Bromine is a chemical element with the symbol Br, and atomic number of 35. It is in the halogen group (17). The element was isolated independently by two chemists, Carl Jacob Löwig and Antoine Jerome Balard, in 1825-1826. Elemental bromine is a fuming red-brown liquid at room temperature, corrosive and toxic, with properties between those of chlorine and iodine. Free bromine does not occur in nature, but occurs as colorless soluble crystalline mineral halide salts, analogous to table salt.

Periodic table

The periodic table is a tabular arrangement of the chemical elements, organized on the basis of their atomic numbers, electron configurations, and recurring chemical properties. Elements are presented in order of increasing atomic number (the number of protons in the nucleus). The standard form of the table consists of a grid of elements laid out in 18 columns and 7 rows, with a double row of elements below that.

Potassium

Potassium is a chemical element with symbol K and atomic number 19. Elemental potassium is a soft silvery-white alkali metal that oxidizes rapidly in air and is very reactive with water, generating sufficient heat to ignite the hydrogen emitted in the reaction and burning with a lilac flame.

Because potassium and sodium are chemically very similar, their salts were not at first differentiated. The existence of multiple elements in their salts was suspected from 1702, and this was proven in 1807 when potassium and sodium were individually isolated from different salts by electrolysis.

4. Atoms and Elements

Straw	Straw is an agricultural by-product, the dry stalks of cereal plants, after the grain and chaff have been removed. Straw makes up about half of the yield of cereal crops such as barley, oats, rice, rye and wheat. It has many uses, including fuel, livestock bedding and fodder, thatching and basket -making.
Americium	Americium is a transuranic radioactive chemical element that has the symbol Am and atomic number 95 Americium was first produced in 1944 by the group of Glenn T. Seaborg at the University of California, Berkeley. Although it is the third element in the transuranic series, it was discovered fourth, after the heavier curium. The discovery was kept secret and only released to the public in November 1945. Most americium is produced by bombarding uranium or plutonium with neutrons in nuclear reactors - one tonne of spent nuclear fuel contains about 100 grams of americium.
Curie	The curie is a non-SI unit of radioactivity the curie is widely used throughout the US government and industry. One curie is roughly the activity of 1 gram of the radium isotope ^{226}Ra, a substance studied by the Curies. The SI derived unit of radioactivity is the becquerel (Bq), which equates to one decay per second.
Curium	Curium is a transuranic radioactive chemical element with the symbol Cm and atomic number 96. This element of the actinide series was named after Marie Sklodowska-Curie and Pierre Curie - both were known for their research on radioactivity. Curium was first intentionally produced and identified in July 1944 by the group of Glenn T. Seaborg at the University of California, Berkeley. The discovery was kept secret and only released to the public in November 1945. Most curium is produced by bombarding uranium or plutonium with neutrons in nuclear reactors - one tonne of spent nuclear fuel contains about 20 grams of curium.
Francium	Francium is a chemical element with symbol Fr and atomic number 87. It was formerly known as eka-caesium and actinium K. It is one of the two least electronegative elements, the other being caesium. Francium is a highly radioactive metal that decays into astatine, radium, and radon. As an alkali metal, it has one valence electron.
Mendelevium	Mendelevium is a synthetic element with the symbol Md and the atomic number 101. A metallic radioactive transuranic element in the actinide series, mendelevium is usually synthesized by bombarding einsteinium with alpha particles. It was named after Dmitri Ivanovich Mendeleev, who created the periodic table, the standard way to classify all the chemical elements.
Polonium	Polonium is a chemical element with the symbol Po and atomic number 84, discovered in 1898 by Marie Curie and Pierre Curie.

A rare and highly radioactive element with no stable isotopes, polonium is chemically similar to bismuth and tellurium, and it occurs in uranium ores. Applications of polonium are few, and include heaters in space probes, antistatic devices, and sources of neutrons and alpha particles.

Chromium

Chromium is a chemical element which has the symbol Cr and atomic number 24. It is the first element in Group 6. It is a steely-gray, lustrous, hard and brittle metal which takes a high polish, resists tarnishing, and has a high melting point. The name of the element is derived from the Greek word 'chroma' (???µa), meaning colour, because many of its compounds are intensely coloured.

Chromium oxide was used by the Chinese in the Qin dynasty over 2,000 years ago to coat metal weapons found with the Terracotta Army.

Germanium

Germanium is a chemical element with symbol Ge and atomic number 32. It is a lustrous, hard, grayish-white metalloid in the carbon group, chemically similar to its group neighbors tin and silicon. Purified germanium is a semiconductor, with an appearance most similar to elemental silicon. Like silicon, germanium naturally reacts and forms complexes with oxygen in nature.

Metalloid

A metalloid is a chemical element that has properties that are in between or a mixture of those of metals and nonmetals and is consequently difficult to classify unambiguously as either a metal or a nonmetal. There is no standard definition of a metalloid, nor is there agreement as to which elements are appropriately classified as such. Despite this lack of specificity the term remains in use in chemistry literature.

Nonmetal

In chemistry, a nonmetal or non-metal is a chemical element which mostly lacks metallic attributes. Physically, nonmetals tend to be highly volatile (easily vaporised), have low elasticity, and are good insulators of heat and electricity; chemically, they tend to have high ionisation energy and electronegativity values, and gain or share electrons when they react with other elements or compounds. Seventeen elements are generally classified as nonmetals; most are gases (hydrogen, helium, nitrogen, oxygen, fluorine, neon, chlorine, argon, krypton, xenon and radon); one is a liquid (bromine); and a few are solids (carbon, phosphorus, sulfur, selenium, and iodine).

Arsenic

Arsenic is a chemical element with symbol As and atomic number 33. Arsenic occurs in many minerals, usually in conjunction with sulfur and metals, and also as a pure elemental crystal. It was first documented by Albertus Magnus in 1250. Arsenic is a metalloid. It can exist in various allotropes, although only the gray form has important use in industry.

Semiconductor

A semiconductor is a material which has electrical conductivity to a degree between that of a metal and that of an insulator (such as glass). Semiconductors are the foundation of modern electronics, including transistors, solar cells, light-emitting diodes (LEDs), quantum dots and digital and analog integrated circuits.

4. Atoms and Elements

CHAPTER HIGHLIGHTS & NOTES: KEY TERMS, PEOPLE, PLACES, CONCEPTS

Algebra

Algebra is one of the broad parts of mathematics, together with number theory, geometry and analysis. As such, it includes everything from elementary equation solving to the study of abstractions such as groups, rings, and fields. The more basic parts of algebra are called elementary algebra, the more abstract parts are called abstract algebra or modern algebra.

Alkali metal

The alkali metals are a group in the periodic table consisting of the chemical elements lithium, sodium (Na), potassium (K), rubidium (Rb), caesium (Cs), and francium (Fr). This group lies in the s-block of the periodic table as all alkali metals have their outermost electron in an s-orbital. The alkali metals provide the best example of group trends in properties in the periodic table, with elements exhibiting well-characterized homologous behaviour.

Alkaline earth metal

The alkaline earth metals are a group of chemical elements in the periodic table with very similar properties. They are all shiny, silvery-white, somewhat reactive metals at standard temperature and pressure and readily lose their two outermost electrons to form cations with charge 2+ and an oxidation state, or oxidation number of +2. In the modern IUPAC nomenclature, the alkaline earth metals comprise the group 2 elements.

The alkaline earth metals are beryllium (Be), magnesium (Mg), calcium (Ca), strontium (Sr), barium (Ba), and radium (Ra).

Barium

Barium is a chemical element with symbol Ba and atomic number 56. It is the fifth element in Group 2, a soft silvery metallic alkaline earth metal. Because of its high chemical reactivity barium is never found in nature as a free element. Its hydroxide was known in pre-modern history as baryta; this substance does not occur as a mineral, but can be prepared by heating barium carbonate.

Calcium

Calcium is the chemical element with symbol Ca and atomic number 20. Calcium is a soft gray alkaline earth metal, and is the fifth-most-abundant element by mass in the Earth's crust. Calcium is also the fifth-most-abundant dissolved ion in seawater by both molarity and mass, after sodium, chloride, magnesium, and sulfate.

Calcium is essential for living organisms, in particular in cell physiology, where movement of the calcium ion Ca^{2+} into and out of the cytoplasm functions as a signal for many cellular processes.

Fluorine

Fluorine is the chemical element with symbol F and atomic number 9. At room temperature, the element is a pale yellow gas composed of diatomic molecules, F2. Fluorine is the lightest halogen and the most electronegative element. It requires great care in handling as it is extremely reactive and poisonous.

Ground state

The ground state of a quantum mechanical system is its lowest-energy state; the energy of the ground state is known as the zero-point energy of the system. An excited state is any state with energy greater than the ground state.

Halogen

The halogens or halogen elements are a group in the periodic table consisting of five chemically related elements, fluorine, chlorine (Cl), bromine (Br), iodine (I), and astatine (At). The artificially created element 117 (ununseptium) may also be a halogen. In the modern IUPAC nomenclature, this group is known as group 17.

Krypton

Krypton is a chemical element with symbol Kr and atomic number 36. It is a member of group 18 (noble gases) elements. A colorless, odorless, tasteless noble gas, krypton occurs in trace amounts in the atmosphere, is isolated by fractionally distilling liquified air, and is often used with other rare gases in fluorescent lamps. Krypton is inert for most practical purposes.

Lithium

Lithium is a chemical element with symbol Li and atomic number 3. It is a soft, silver-white metal belonging to the alkali metal group of chemical elements. Under standard conditions it is the lightest metal and the least dense solid element. Like all alkali metals, lithium is highly reactive and flammable.

Rubidium

Rubidium is a chemical element with the symbol Rb and atomic number 37. Rubidium is a soft, silvery-white metallic element of the alkali metal group, with an atomic mass of 85.4678. Elemental rubidium is highly reactive, with properties similar to those of other alkali metals, such as very rapid oxidation in air. Natural rubidium is a mix of two isotopes: ^{85}Rb, the only stable one, constitutes 72% of it, and 28% is accounted for slightly radioactive ^{87}Rb with a half-life of 49 billion years--more than three times longer than the estimated age of the universe.

German chemists Robert Bunsen and Gustav Kirchhoff discovered rubidium in 1861 by the newly developed method of flame spectroscopy.

Strontium

Strontium is a chemical element with symbol Sr and atomic number 38. An alkaline earth metal, strontium is a soft silver-white or yellowish metallic element that is highly reactive chemically. The metal turns yellow when it is exposed to air. Strontium has physical and chemical properties similar to those of its two neighbors calcium and barium.

Xenon

Xenon is a chemical element with the symbol Xe and atomic number 54. It is a colorless, heavy, odorless noble gas, that occurs in the Earth's atmosphere in trace amounts. Although generally unreactive, xenon can undergo a few chemical reactions such as the formation of xenon hexafluoroplatinate, the first noble gas compound to be synthesized.

Naturally occurring xenon consists of eight stable isotopes.

Alkali

In chemistry, an alkali is a basic, ionic salt of an alkali metal or alkaline earth metal chemical element. Some authors also define an alkali as a base that dissolves in water. A solution of a soluble base has a pH greater than 7.0. The adjective alkaline is commonly, and alkalescent less often, used in English as a synonym for basic, especially for soluble bases.

4. Atoms and Elements

CHAPTER HIGHLIGHTS & NOTES: KEY TERMS, PEOPLE, PLACES, CONCEPTS

Chloride ion	The chloride ion is the anion Cl^-. It is formed when the element chlorine (a halogen) gains an electron or when a compound such as hydrogen chloride is dissolved in water or other polar solvents. Chlorides salts such as sodium chloride are often very soluble in water.
Sodium	Sodium is a chemical element with the symbol Na and atomic number 11. It is a soft, silver-white, highly reactive metal and is a member of the alkali metals; its only stable isotope is ^{23}Na. The free metal does not occur in nature, but instead must be prepared from its compounds; it was first isolated by Humphry Davy in 1807 by the electrolysis of sodium hydroxide. Sodium is the sixth most abundant element in the Earth's crust, and exists in numerous minerals such as feldspars, sodalite and rock salt.
Sodium chloride	Sodium chloride, also known as salt, common salt, table salt or halite, is an ionic compound with the formula NaCl, representing equal proportions of sodium and chlorine. Sodium chloride is the salt most responsible for the salinity of the ocean and of the extracellular fluid of many multicellular organisms. As the major ingredient in edible salt, it is commonly used as a condiment and food preservative.
Valence electron	In chemistry, a valence electron is an electron that is associated with an atom, and that can participate in the formation of a chemical bond; in a single covalent bond, both atoms in the bond contribute one valence electron in order to form a shared pair. The presence of valence electrons can determine the element's chemical properties and whether it may bond with other elements: For a main group element, a valence electron can only be in the outermost electron shell. In a transition metal, a valence electron can also be in an inner shell.
Beryllium	Beryllium is the chemical element with the symbol Be and atomic number 4. Because any beryllium synthesized in stars is short-lived, it is a relatively rare element in both the universe and in the crust of the Earth. It is a divalent element which occurs naturally only in combination with other elements in minerals. Notable gemstones which contain beryllium include beryl (aquamarine, emerald) and chrysoberyl.
Chloride	The chloride ion is formed when the element chlorine gains an electron to form an anion (negatively charged ion) Cl^-. The salts of hydrochloric acid contain chloride ions and can also be called chlorides. The chloride ion, and its salts such as sodium chloride, are very soluble in water.
Isotope	Isotopes are variants of a particular chemical element such that, while all isotopes of a given element have the same number of protons in each atom, they differ in neutron number. The term isotope is formed from the Greek roots isos (?s?? 'equal') and topos (t?p?? 'place'), meaning 'the same place'. Thus, different isotopes of a single element occupy the same position on the periodic table.
Mass number	The mass number, also called atomic mass number or nucleon number, is the total number of protons and neutrons (together known as nucleons) in an atomic nucleus.

Because protons and neutrons both are baryons, the mass number A is identical with the baryon number B as of the nucleus as of the whole atom or ion. The mass number is different for each different isotope of a chemical element.

CHAPTER QUIZ: KEY TERMS, PEOPLE, PLACES, CONCEPTS

1. In chemistry, an _________ is a basic, ionic salt of an _________ metal or alkaline earth metal chemical element. Some authors also define an _________ as a base that dissolves in water. A solution of a soluble base has a pH greater than 7.0. The adjective alkaline is commonly, and alkalescent less often, used in English as a synonym for basic, especially for soluble bases.

   a. 18-Electron rule
   b. Crucible
   c. Cross-validation
   d. Alkali

2. _________ is a chemical element with symbol Ba and atomic number 56. It is the fifth element in Group 2, a soft silvery metallic alkaline earth metal. Because of its high chemical reactivity _________ is never found in nature as a free element. Its hydroxide was known in pre-modern history as baryta; this substance does not occur as a mineral, but can be prepared by heating _________ carbonate.

   a. Chemical element
   b. Systematic element name
   c. Barium
   d. Lidar

3. . In chemistry and physics, _________ is a scientific theory of the nature of matter, which states that matter is composed of discrete units called atoms, as opposed to the earlier concept which held that matter could be divided into any arbitrarily small quantity. It began as a philosophical concept in ancient Greece (Democritus) and entered the scientific mainstream in the early 19th century when discoveries in the field of chemistry showed that matter did indeed behave as if it were made up of particles.

   The word 'atom' (from the ancient Greek adjective atomos, 'indivisible'.

   a. Cotton effect
   b. Core electron
   c. Atomic theory

4. The _________ is a non-SI unit of radioactivity the _________ is widely used throughout the US government and industry.

   One _________ is roughly the activity of 1 gram of the radium isotope ^{226}Ra, a substance studied by the _________s.

   The SI derived unit of radioactivity is the becquerel (Bq), which equates to one decay per second.

   a. 5 yen coin
   b. Background radiation
   c. Curie
   d. Bateman Equation

5. In atomic physics, the _________, introduced by Niels Bohr in 1913, depicts the atom as small, positively charged nucleus surrounded by electrons that travel in circular orbits around the nucleus--similar in structure to the solar system, but with attraction provided by electrostatic forces rather than gravity. After the cubic model .•Quantum ruleThe angular momentum L = $m_e$vr is an integer multiple of h: $m_e vr = n\hbar$ Substituting the expression for the velocity gives an equation for r in terms of n: $\sqrt{Zk_e e^2 m_e r} = n\hbar$ so that the allowed orbit radius at any n is: $r_n = \frac{n^2\hbar^2}{Zk_e e^2 m_e}$ The smallest possible value of r in the hydrogen atom is called the Bohr radius and is equal to: $r_1 = \frac{\hbar^2}{k_e e^2 m_e} \approx 5.29 \times 10^{-11}\mathrm{m}$ The energy of the n-th level for any atom is determined by the radius and quantum number: $E = -\frac{Zk_e e^2}{2r_n} = -\frac{Z^2(k_e e^2)^2 m_e}{2\hbar^2 n^2} \approx \frac{-13.6Z^2}{n^2}\mathrm{eV}$

   An electron in the lowest energy level of hydrogen therefore has about 13.6 eV less energy than a motionless electron infinitely far from the nucleus. The next energy level is -3.4 eV. The third (n = 3) is -1.51 eV, and so on.

   a. Bohr model
   b. Cotton effect
   c. Core electron
   d. Double ionization

ANSWER KEY
4. Atoms and Elements

---

1. d
2. c
3. c
4. c
5. a

---

5. Molecules and Compounds

CHAPTER OUTLINE: KEY TERMS, PEOPLE, PLACES, CONCEPTS

- Lewis structure
- Sodium
- Sodium chloride
- Ammonia
- Decomposition
- Carbon dioxide
- Carbon monoxide
- Polyatomic ion
- Ball-and-stick model
- Hydrogen peroxide
- Molecular model
- Space-filling model
- Diatomic molecule
- Helium
- Mendelevium
- Molar volume
- Oxygen
- Diatomic
- Acetone
- Dry ice
- Ionic compound

5. Molecules and Compounds

CHAPTER OUTLINE: KEY TERMS, PEOPLE, PLACES, CONCEPTS

- Monatomic ion
- Oxide
- Magnesium oxide
- Ammonium nitrate
- Nitrite
- Oxyanion
- Potassium nitrate
- Calcium carbonate
- Hypochlorite
- Perchlorate
- Sodium bicarbonate
- Sodium nitrite
- Binary acid
- Hydrobromic acid
- Hydrochloric acid
- Nitric acid
- Sulfurous acid
- Limestone
- Algebra
- Alkali metal
- Alkali

5. Molecules and Compounds

CHAPTER OUTLINE: KEY TERMS, PEOPLE, PLACES, CONCEPTS

	Radiation
	Atomic mass

CHAPTER HIGHLIGHTS & NOTES: KEY TERMS, PEOPLE, PLACES, CONCEPTS

Lewis structure	Lewis structures are diagrams that show the bonding between atoms of a molecule and the lone pairs of electrons that may exist in the molecule. A Lewis structure can be drawn for any covalently bonded molecule, as well as coordination compounds. The Lewis structure was named after Gilbert N
Sodium	Sodium is a chemical element with the symbol Na and atomic number 11. It is a soft, silver-white, highly reactive metal and is a member of the alkali metals; its only stable isotope is ^{23}Na. The free metal does not occur in nature, but instead must be prepared from its compounds; it was first isolated by Humphry Davy in 1807 by the electrolysis of sodium hydroxide. Sodium is the sixth most abundant element in the Earth's crust, and exists in numerous minerals such as feldspars, sodalite and rock salt.
Sodium chloride	Sodium chloride, also known as salt, common salt, table salt or halite, is an ionic compound with the formula NaCl, representing equal proportions of sodium and chlorine. Sodium chloride is the salt most responsible for the salinity of the ocean and of the extracellular fluid of many multicellular organisms. As the major ingredient in edible salt, it is commonly used as a condiment and food preservative.
Ammonia	Ammonia or azane is a compound of nitrogen and hydrogen with the formula NH_3. It is a colourless gas with a characteristic pungent smell. Ammonia contributes significantly to the nutritional needs of terrestrial organisms by serving as a precursor to food and fertilizers.
Decomposition	Decomposition is the process by which organic substances are broken down into simpler forms of matter. The process is essential for recycling the finite matter that occupies physical space in the biome. Bodies of living organisms begin to decompose shortly after death.
Carbon dioxide	Carbon dioxide is a naturally occurring chemical compound composed of two oxygen atoms each covalently double bonded to a single carbon atom. It is a gas at standard temperature and pressure and exists in Earth's atmosphere in this state, as a trace gas at a concentration of 0.039 per cent by volume.

5. Molecules and Compounds

CHAPTER HIGHLIGHTS & NOTES: KEY TERMS, PEOPLE, PLACES, CONCEPTS

Carbon monoxide	Carbon monoxide is a colorless, odorless, and tasteless gas that is slightly less dense than air. It is toxic to humans and animals when encountered in higher concentrations, although it is also produced in normal animal metabolism in low quantities, and is thought to have some normal biological functions. In the atmosphere, it is spatially variable, short lived, having a role in the formation of ground-level ozone.
Polyatomic ion	A polyatomic ion, also known as a molecular ion, is a charged chemical species composed of two or more atoms covalently bonded or of a metal complex that can be considered to be acting as a single unit. The prefix 'poly-' means 'many,' in Greek, but even ions of two atoms are commonly referred to as polyatomic. In older literature, a polyatomic ion is also referred to as a radical, and less commonly, as a radical group.
Ball-and-stick model	In chemistry, the ball-and-stick model is a molecular model of a chemical substance which is to display both the three-dimensional position of the atoms and the bonds between them. The atoms are typically represented by spheres, connected by rods which represent the bonds. Double and triple bonds are usually represented by two or three curved rods, respectively.
Hydrogen peroxide	Hydrogen peroxide is the simplest peroxide (a compound with an oxygen-oxygen single bond). It is also a strong oxidizer. Hydrogen peroxide is a clear liquid, slightly more viscous than water.
Molecular model	A molecular model, in this article, is a physical model that represents molecules and their processes. The creation of mathematical models of molecular properties and behaviour is molecular modelling, and their graphical depiction is molecular graphics, but these topics are closely linked and each uses techniques from the others. In this article, 'molecular model' will primarily refer to systems containing more than one atom and where nuclear structure is neglected.
Space-filling model	In chemistry, a space-filling model, also known as a calotte model, is a type of three-dimensional molecular model where the atoms are represented by spheres whose radii are proportional to the radii of the atoms and whose center-to-center distances are proportional to the distances between the atomic nuclei, all in the same scale. Atoms of different chemical elements are usually represented by spheres of different colors. Calotte models are distinguished from other 3D representations, such as the ball-and-stick and skeletal models, by the use of 'full size' balls for the atoms.
Diatomic molecule	Diatomic molecules are molecules composed only of two atoms, of either the same or different chemical elements. The prefix di- is of Greek origin, meaning two.
Helium	Helium is a chemical element with symbol He and atomic number 2. It is a colorless, odorless, tasteless, non-toxic, inert, monatomic gas that heads the noble gas group in the periodic table. Its boiling and melting points are the lowest among the elements and it exists only as a gas except in extreme conditions.

Mendelevium	Mendelevium is a synthetic element with the symbol Md and the atomic number 101. A metallic radioactive transuranic element in the actinide series, mendelevium is usually synthesized by bombarding einsteinium with alpha particles. It was named after Dmitri Ivanovich Mendeleev, who created the periodic table, the standard way to classify all the chemical elements.
Molar volume	The molar volume, symbol V_m, is the volume occupied by one mole of a substance at a given temperature and pressure. It is equal to the molar mass (M) divided by the mass density (?). It has the SI unit cubic metres per mole (m^3/mol), although it is more practical to use the units cubic decimetres per mole (dm^3/mol) for gases and cubic centimetres per mole (cm^3/mol) for liquids and solids.
Oxygen	Oxygen is a chemical element with symbol O and atomic number 8. It is a member of the chalcogen group on the periodic table and is a highly reactive nonmetallic element and oxidizing agent that readily forms compounds (notably oxides) with most elements. By mass, oxygen is the third-most abundant element in the universe, after hydrogen and helium At STP, two atoms of the element bind to form dioxygen, a diatomic gas that is colorless, odorless, and tasteless; with the formula O2. Many major classes of organic molecules in living organisms, such as proteins, nucleic acids, carbohydrates, and fats, contain oxygen, as do the major inorganic compounds that are constituents of animal shells, teeth, and bone.
Diatomic	Diatomic molecules are molecules composed of only two atoms, of either the same or different chemical elements. The prefix di- is of Greek origin, meaning 'two'. If a diatomic molecule consists of two atoms of the same element, such as hydrogen (H_2) or oxygen (O_2), then it is said to be homonuclear.
Acetone	Acetone is the organic compound with the formula $(CH_3)_2CO$. It is a colorless, mobile, flammable liquid, and is the simplest ketone. Acetone is miscible with water and serves as an important solvent in its own right, typically for cleaning purposes in the laboratory. About 6.7 million tonnes were produced worldwide in 2010, mainly for use as a solvent and production of methyl methacrylate and bisphenol A. It is a common building block in organic chemistry.
Dry ice	Dry ice, sometimes referred to as 'cardice' or as 'card ice', is the solid form of carbon dioxide. It is used primarily as a cooling agent. Its advantages include lower temperature than that of water ice and not leaving any residue (other than incidental frost from moisture in the atmosphere).
Ionic compound	In chemistry, an ionic compound is a chemical compound in which ions are held together in a lattice structure by ionic bonds.

Usually, the positively charged portion consists of metal cations and the negatively charged portion is an anion or polyatomic ion. Ions in ionic compounds are held together by the electrostatic forces between oppositely charged bodies.

Monatomic ion

A monatomic ion is an ion consisting of a single atom. If an ion contains more than 1 atom, even if these atoms are of the same element, it is called a polyatomic ion. For example calcium carbonate consists of the monatomic ion Ca^{2+} and the polyatomic ion CO_3^{2-}.

Oxide

An oxide is a chemical compound that contains at least one oxygen atom and one other element in its chemical formula. Metal oxides typically contain an anion of oxygen in the oxidation state of -2. Most of the Earth's crust consists of solid oxides, the result of elements being oxidized by the oxygen in air or in water. Hydrocarbon combustion affords the two principal carbon oxides: carbon monoxide and carbon dioxide.

Magnesium oxide

Magnesium oxide, or magnesia, is a white hygroscopic solid mineral that occurs naturally as periclase and is a source of magnesium . It has an empirical formula of MgO and consists of a lattice of Mg^{2+} ions and O^{2-} ions held together by ionic bonding. Magnesium hydroxide forms in the presence of water ($MgO + H_2O$? $Mg(OH)_2$), but it can be reversed by heating it to separate moisture.

Ammonium nitrate

The chemical compound ammonium nitrate, the nitrate of ammonia with the chemical formula NH_4NO_3, is a white crystalline solid at room temperature and standard pressure. It is commonly used in agriculture as a high-nitrogen fertilizer, and it has also been used as an oxidizing agent in explosives, including improvised explosive devices. It is the main component of ANFO, a popular explosive, which accounts for 80% explosives used in North America. It is used in instant cold packs, as hydrating the salt is an endothermic process.

Nitrite

The nitrite ion, which has the chemical formula NO_2^-, is a symmetric anion with equal N-O bond lengths and an O-N-O bond angle of approximately 120°. Upon protonation, the unstable weak acid nitrous acid is produced. Nitrite can be oxidized or reduced, with the product somewhat dependent on the oxidizing/reducing agent and its strength.

Oxyanion

An oxyanion or oxoanion is a chemical compound with the generic formula $A_xO_y^{z-}$. Oxoanions are formed by a large majority of the chemical elements. The formulae of simple oxoanions are determined by the octet rule.

Potassium nitrate

Potassium nitrate is a chemical compound with the formula KNO_3. It is an ionic salt of potassium ions K^+ and nitrate ions NO_3^-.

Calcium carbonate	Calcium carbonate is a chemical compound with the formula $CaCO_3$. It is a common substance found in rocks in all parts of the world, and is the main component of shells of marine organisms, snails, coal balls, pearls, and eggshells. Calcium carbonate is the active ingredient in agricultural lime, and is created when Ca ions in hard water react with carbonate ions creating limescale.
Hypochlorite	In chemistry, hypochlorite is an ion composed of chlorine and oxygen, with the chemical formula ClO^-. It can combine with a number of counter ions to form hypochlorites, which may also be regarded as the salts of hypochlorous acid. Common examples include sodium hypochlorite and calcium hypochlorite.
Perchlorate	Perchlorates are the salts derived from perchloric acid--in particular when referencing the polyatomic anions found in solution, perchlorate is often written with the formula ClO_4^-. Perchlorates are often produced by natural processes but can also be produced artificially. They have been used for more than fifty years to treat thyroid disorders.
Sodium bicarbonate	Sodium bicarbonate or sodium hydrogen carbonate is the chemical compound with the formula $NaHCO_3$. Sodium bicarbonate is a white solid that is crystalline but often appears as a fine powder. It has a slightly salty, alkaline taste resembling that of washing soda (sodium carbonate).
Sodium nitrite	Sodium nitrite is the inorganic compound with the chemical formula $NaNO_2$. It is a white to slight yellowish crystalline powder that is very soluble in water and is hygroscopic. It is a useful precursor to a variety of organic compounds, such as pharmaceuticals, dyes, and pesticides, but it is probably best known as a food additive to prevent botulism.
Binary acid	Binary acids are certain molecular compounds in which hydrogen is combined with a second nonmetallic element. Examples:•HF•HCl•HBr•HI Their strengths depend on the solvation of the initial acid, the H-X bond energy, the electron affinity energy of X, and the solvation energy of X. Observed trends in acidity correlate with bond energies, the weaker the H-X bond, the stronger the acid. For example, there is a weak bond between hydrogen and iodine in hydroiodic acid, making it a very strong acid.
Hydrobromic acid	Hydrobromic acid is a strong acid formed by dissolving the diatomic molecule hydrogen bromide in water. 'Constant boiling' hydrobromic acid is an aqueous solution that distills at 124.3 °C and contains 47.6% HBr by weight, which is 8.89 mol/L. Hydrobromic acid has a pK_a of -9, making it a stronger acid than hydrochloric acid, but not as strong as hydroiodic acid. Hydrobromic acid is one of the strongest mineral acids known.
Hydrochloric acid	Hydrochloric acid is a clear, colorless, highly pungent solution of hydrogen chloride in water.

It is a highly corrosive, strong mineral acid with many industrial uses. Hydrochloric acid is found naturally in gastric acid.

Nitric acid

Nitric acid, also known as aqua fortis and spirit of niter, is a highly corrosive strong mineral acid. The pure compound is colorless, but older samples tend to acquire a yellow cast due to decomposition into oxides of nitrogen and water. Most commercially available nitric acid has a concentration of 68%.

Sulfurous acid

Sulfurous acid is the chemical compound with the formula H_2SO_3. There is no evidence that sulfurous acid exists in solution, but the molecule has been detected in the gas phase. The conjugate bases of this elusive acid are, however, common anions, bisulfite (or hydrogensulfite) and sulfite.

Limestone

Limestone is a sedimentary rock composed largely of the minerals calcite and aragonite, which are different crystal forms of calcium carbonate . Many limestones are composed from skeletal fragments of marine organisms such as coral or foraminifera.

Limestone makes up about 10% of the total volume of all sedimentary rocks.

Algebra

Algebra is one of the broad parts of mathematics, together with number theory, geometry and analysis. As such, it includes everything from elementary equation solving to the study of abstractions such as groups, rings, and fields. The more basic parts of algebra are called elementary algebra, the more abstract parts are called abstract algebra or modern algebra.

Alkali metal

The alkali metals are a group in the periodic table consisting of the chemical elements lithium, sodium (Na), potassium (K), rubidium (Rb), caesium (Cs), and francium (Fr). This group lies in the s-block of the periodic table as all alkali metals have their outermost electron in an s-orbital. The alkali metals provide the best example of group trends in properties in the periodic table, with elements exhibiting well-characterized homologous behaviour.

Alkali

In chemistry, an alkali is a basic, ionic salt of an alkali metal or alkaline earth metal chemical element. Some authors also define an alkali as a base that dissolves in water. A solution of a soluble base has a pH greater than 7.0. The adjective alkaline is commonly, and alkalescent less often, used in English as a synonym for basic, especially for soluble bases.

Radiation

In physics, radiation is a process in which energetic particles or energetic waves travel through a vacuum, or through matter-containing media that are not required for their propagation. Waves of a mass filled medium itself, such as water waves or sound waves, are usually not considered to be forms of 'radiation' in this sense.

CHAPTER HIGHLIGHTS & NOTES: KEY TERMS, PEOPLE, PLACES, CONCEPTS

Atomic mass	The atomic mass is the mass of an atomic particle, sub-atomic particle, or molecule. It may be expressed in unified atomic mass units; by international agreement, 1 atomic mass unit is defined as 1/12 of the mass of a single carbon-12 atom (at rest). When expressed in such units, the atomic mass is called the relative isotopic mass .

CHAPTER QUIZ: KEY TERMS, PEOPLE, PLACES, CONCEPTS

1. The chemical compound _________, the nitrate of ammonia with the chemical formula NH_4NO_3, is a white crystalline solid at room temperature and standard pressure. It is commonly used in agriculture as a high-nitrogen fertilizer, and it has also been used as an oxidizing agent in explosives, including improvised explosive devices. It is the main component of ANFO, a popular explosive, which accounts for 80% explosives used in North America. It is used in instant cold packs, as hydrating the salt is an endothermic process.

   a. Binder
   b. Bioadhesive
   c. Blu-Tack
   d. Ammonium nitrate

2. A _________, also known as a molecular ion, is a charged chemical species composed of two or more atoms covalently bonded or of a metal complex that can be considered to be acting as a single unit. The prefix 'poly-' means 'many,' in Greek, but even ions of two atoms are commonly referred to as polyatomic. In older literature, a _________ is also referred to as a radical, and less commonly, as a radical group.

   a. Polyatomic ion
   b. Dication
   c. Distonic ion
   d. Liquid junction interface

3. _________, sometimes referred to as 'cardice' or as 'card ice', is the solid form of carbon dioxide. It is used primarily as a cooling agent. Its advantages include lower temperature than that of water ice and not leaving any residue (other than incidental frost from moisture in the atmosphere).

   a. Dry ice
   b. Cerimetry
   c. Bradford protein assay
   d. Bulk material analyzer

4. . _________ is a chemical element with the symbol Na and atomic number 11.

5. Molecules and Compounds

It is a soft, silver-white, highly reactive metal and is a member of the alkali metals; its only stable isotope is ^{23}Na. The free metal does not occur in nature, but instead must be prepared from its compounds; it was first isolated by Humphry Davy in 1807 by the electrolysis of _________ hydroxide. _________ is the sixth most abundant element in the Earth's crust, and exists in numerous minerals such as feldspars, sodalite and rock salt.

a. Clarkeite
b. Sodium
c. Hydrohalite
d. Magadiite

5. _________ or azane is a compound of nitrogen and hydrogen with the formula NH_3. It is a colourless gas with a characteristic pungent smell. _________ contributes significantly to the nutritional needs of terrestrial organisms by serving as a precursor to food and fertilizers.

a. Barium acetylacetonate
b. Cerium acetylacetonate
c. Ammonia
d. Gadolinium acetylacetonate

ANSWER KEY
5. Molecules and Compounds

1. d
2. a
3. a
4. b
5. c

---

6. Chemical Composition

CHAPTER OUTLINE: KEY TERMS, PEOPLE, PLACES, CONCEPTS

- Sodium chloride
- Chloride
- Sodium
- Iron ore
- Avogadro
- Bohr model
- Electron
- Helium
- Atom
- Mole
- Lithium
- Carbon
- Ionic compound
- Molecule
- Dry ice
- Carbon dioxide
- Lewis structure
- Chloride ion
- Ozone
- Chlorine
- Chlorofluorocarbon

6. Chemical Composition

CHAPTER OUTLINE: KEY TERMS, PEOPLE, PLACES, CONCEPTS

	Chromium
	Mass number
	Fluoride
	Hydrogen peroxide
	Water fluoridation
	Experimental data
	Decomposition

CHAPTER HIGHLIGHTS & NOTES: KEY TERMS, PEOPLE, PLACES, CONCEPTS

Sodium chloride	Sodium chloride, also known as salt, common salt, table salt or halite, is an ionic compound with the formula NaCl, representing equal proportions of sodium and chlorine. Sodium chloride is the salt most responsible for the salinity of the ocean and of the extracellular fluid of many multicellular organisms. As the major ingredient in edible salt, it is commonly used as a condiment and food preservative.
Chloride	The chloride ion is formed when the element chlorine gains an electron to form an anion (negatively charged ion) Cl^-. The salts of hydrochloric acid contain chloride ions and can also be called chlorides. The chloride ion, and its salts such as sodium chloride, are very soluble in water.
Sodium	Sodium is a chemical element with the symbol Na and atomic number 11. It is a soft, silver-white, highly reactive metal and is a member of the alkali metals; its only stable isotope is ^{23}Na. The free metal does not occur in nature, but instead must be prepared from its compounds; it was first isolated by Humphry Davy in 1807 by the electrolysis of sodium hydroxide. Sodium is the sixth most abundant element in the Earth's crust, and exists in numerous minerals such as feldspars, sodalite and rock salt.
Iron ore	Iron ores are rocks and minerals from which metallic iron can be economically extracted. The ores are usually rich in iron oxides and vary in color from dark grey, bright yellow, deep purple, to rusty red. The iron itself is usually found in the form of magnetite (Fe3O4), hematite (Fe2O

Avogadro

Avogadro is a molecular editor designed for cross-platform use in computational chemistry, molecular modeling, bioinformatics, materials science, and related areas. It is extensible through a plugin architecture.

Bohr model

In atomic physics, the Bohr model, introduced by Niels Bohr in 1913, depicts the atom as small, positively charged nucleus surrounded by electrons that travel in circular orbits around the nucleus--similar in structure to the solar system, but with attraction provided by electrostatic forces rather than gravity. After the cubic model .•Quantum ruleThe angular momentum L = $m_e$vr is an integer multiple of h: $m_e v r = n\hbar$ Substituting the expression for the velocity gives an equation for r in terms of n: $\sqrt{Zk_e e^2 m_e r} = n\hbar$ so that the allowed orbit radius at any n is: $r_n = \frac{n^2\hbar^2}{Zk_e e^2 m_e}$ The smallest possible value of r in the hydrogen atom is called the Bohr radius and is equal to: $r_1 = \frac{\hbar^2}{k_e e^2 m_e} \approx 5.29 \times 10^{-11}\mathrm{m}$ The energy of the n-th level for any atom is determined by the radius and quantum number: $E = -\frac{Zk_e e^2}{2r_n} = -\frac{Z^2(k_e e^2)^2 m_e}{2\hbar^2 n^2} \approx \frac{-13.6Z^2}{n^2}\mathrm{eV}$

An electron in the lowest energy level of hydrogen therefore has about 13.6 eV less energy than a motionless electron infinitely far from the nucleus. The next energy level is -3.4 eV. The third (n = 3) is -1.51 eV, and so on.

Electron

The electron is a subatomic particle with a negative elementary electric charge. Electrons belong to the first generation of the lepton particle family, and are generally thought to be elementary particles because they have no known components or substructure. The electron has a mass that is approximately 1/1836 that of the proton.

Helium

Helium is a chemical element with symbol He and atomic number 2. It is a colorless, odorless, tasteless, non-toxic, inert, monatomic gas that heads the noble gas group in the periodic table. Its boiling and melting points are the lowest among the elements and it exists only as a gas except in extreme conditions.

Helium is the second lightest element and is the second most abundant element in the observable universe, being present at about 24% of the total elemental mass, which is more than 12 times the mass of all the heavier elements combined.

Atom

The atom is a basic unit of matter that consists of a dense central nucleus surrounded by a cloud of negatively charged electrons. The atomic nucleus contains a mix of positively charged protons and electrically neutral neutrons, which means 'uncuttable' or 'the smallest indivisible particle of matter'.

6. Chemical Composition

Mole	Mole is a unit of measurement used in chemistry to express amounts of a chemical substance, defined as the amount of any substance that contains as many elementary entities (e.g., atoms, molecules, ions, electrons) as there are atoms in 12 grams of pure carbon-12, the isotope of carbon with relative atomic mass 12. This corresponds to the Avogadro constant, which has a value of $6.02214129(27)\times10^{23}$ elementary entities of the substance. It is one of the base units in the International System of Units, and has the unit symbol mol and corresponds with the dimension symbol N. In honour of the unit, chemists often celebrate October 23 (a reference to the 10^{23} part of Avogadro's number) as 'Mole Day'. The mole is widely used in chemistry instead of units of mass or volume as a convenient way to express amounts of reactants or of products of chemical reactions.
Lithium	Lithium is a chemical element with symbol Li and atomic number 3. It is a soft, silver-white metal belonging to the alkali metal group of chemical elements. Under standard conditions it is the lightest metal and the least dense solid element. Like all alkali metals, lithium is highly reactive and flammable.
Carbon	Carbon fiber, alternatively graphite fiber, carbon graphite or CF, is a material consisting of fibers about 5-10 μm in diameter and composed mostly of carbon atoms. The carbon atoms are bonded together in crystals that are more or less aligned parallel to the long axis of the fiber. The crystal alignment gives the fiber high strength-to-volume ratio (making it strong for its size).
Ionic compound	In chemistry, an ionic compound is a chemical compound in which ions are held together in a lattice structure by ionic bonds. Usually, the positively charged portion consists of metal cations and the negatively charged portion is an anion or polyatomic ion. Ions in ionic compounds are held together by the electrostatic forces between oppositely charged bodies.
Molecule	A molecule is an electrically neutral group of two or more atoms held together by chemical bonds. Molecules are distinguished from ions by their lack of electrical charge. However, in quantum physics, organic chemistry, and biochemistry, the term molecule is often used less strictly, also being applied to polyatomic ions.
Dry ice	Dry ice, sometimes referred to as 'cardice' or as 'card ice', is the solid form of carbon dioxide. It is used primarily as a cooling agent. Its advantages include lower temperature than that of water ice and not leaving any residue (other than incidental frost from moisture in the atmosphere).
Carbon dioxide	Carbon dioxide is a naturally occurring chemical compound composed of two oxygen atoms each covalently double bonded to a single carbon atom. It is a gas at standard temperature and pressure and exists in Earth's atmosphere in this state, as a trace gas at a concentration of 0.039 per cent by volume.

Lewis structure	Lewis structures are diagrams that show the bonding between atoms of a molecule and the lone pairs of electrons that may exist in the molecule. A Lewis structure can be drawn for any covalently bonded molecule, as well as coordination compounds. The Lewis structure was named after Gilbert N
Chloride ion	The chloride ion is the anion Cl^-. It is formed when the element chlorine (a halogen) gains an electron or when a compound such as hydrogen chloride is dissolved in water or other polar solvents. Chlorides salts such as sodium chloride are often very soluble in water.
Ozone	Ozone, or trioxygen, is an inorganic compound with the chemical formula O3(μ-O) (also written [O (μ-O)O] or O3). It is a pale blue gas with a distinctively pungent smell. It is an allotrope of oxygen that is much less stable than the diatomic allotrope O2, breaking down in the lower atmosphere to normal dioxygen.
Chlorine	Chlorine is a chemical element with symbol Cl and atomic number 17. Chlorine is in the halogen group (17) and is the second lightest halogen after fluorine. The element is a yellow-green gas under standard conditions, where it forms diatomic molecules. It has the highest electron affinity and the fourth highest electronegativity of all the reactive elements; for this reason, chlorine is a strong oxidizing agent.
Chlorofluorocarbon	A chlorofluorocarbon is an organic compound that contains only carbon, chlorine, and fluorine, produced as a volatile derivative of methane and ethane. They are also commonly known by the DuPont brand name Freon. The most common representative is dichlorodifluoromethane (R-12 or Freon-12).
Chromium	Chromium is a chemical element which has the symbol Cr and atomic number 24. It is the first element in Group 6. It is a steely-gray, lustrous, hard and brittle metal which takes a high polish, resists tarnishing, and has a high melting point. The name of the element is derived from the Greek word 'chroma' (???μa), meaning colour, because many of its compounds are intensely coloured. Chromium oxide was used by the Chinese in the Qin dynasty over 2,000 years ago to coat metal weapons found with the Terracotta Army.
Mass number	The mass number, also called atomic mass number or nucleon number, is the total number of protons and neutrons (together known as nucleons) in an atomic nucleus. Because protons and neutrons both are baryons, the mass number A is identical with the baryon number B as of the nucleus as of the whole atom or ion. The mass number is different for each different isotope of a chemical element.
Fluoride	Fluoride is an inorganic anion of fluorine with the chemical formula F-. It contributes no color to fluoride salts.

6. Chemical Composition

CHAPTER HIGHLIGHTS & NOTES: KEY TERMS, PEOPLE, PLACES, CONCEPTS

Hydrogen peroxide	Hydrogen peroxide is the simplest peroxide (a compound with an oxygen-oxygen single bond). It is also a strong oxidizer. Hydrogen peroxide is a clear liquid, slightly more viscous than water.
Water fluoridation	Water fluoridation is the controlled addition of fluoride to a public water supply to reduce tooth decay. Fluoridated water has fluoride at a level that is effective for preventing cavities; this can occur naturally or by adding fluoride. Fluoridated water operates on tooth surfaces: in the mouth it creates low levels of fluoride in saliva, which reduces the rate at which tooth enamel demineralizes and increases the rate at which it remineralizes in the early stages of cavities.
Experimental data	Experimental data in science is data produced by a measurement, test method, experimental design or quasi-experimental design. In clinical research any data produced as a result of clinical trial. Experimental data may be qualitative or quantitative, each being appropriate for different investigations.
Decomposition	Decomposition is the process by which organic substances are broken down into simpler forms of matter. The process is essential for recycling the finite matter that occupies physical space in the biome. Bodies of living organisms begin to decompose shortly after death.

CHAPTER QUIZ: KEY TERMS, PEOPLE, PLACES, CONCEPTS

1. _________, sometimes referred to as 'cardice' or as 'card ice', is the solid form of carbon dioxide. It is used primarily as a cooling agent. Its advantages include lower temperature than that of water ice and not leaving any residue (other than incidental frost from moisture in the atmosphere).

   a. Clathrate hydrate
   b. Cerimetry
   c. Bradford protein assay
   d. Dry ice

2. . _________ is a unit of measurement used in chemistry to express amounts of a chemical substance, defined as the amount of any substance that contains as many elementary entities (e.g., atoms, molecules, ions, electrons) as there are atoms in 12 grams of pure carbon-12, the isotope of carbon with relative atomic mass 12. This corresponds to the Avogadro constant, which has a value of $6.02214129(27)\times10^{23}$ elementary entities of the substance. It is one of the base units in the International System of Units, and has the unit symbol mol and corresponds with the dimension symbol N. In honour of the unit, chemists often celebrate October 23 (a reference to the 10^{23} part of Avogadro's number) as '_________ Day'.

   The _________ is widely used in chemistry instead of units of mass or volume as a convenient way to express amounts of reactants or of products of chemical reactions.

a. Mole
b. Kilogram per cubic metre
c. Bisulfide
d. Buffering agent

3. _________ is the process by which organic substances are broken down into simpler forms of matter. The process is essential for recycling the finite matter that occupies physical space in the biome. Bodies of living organisms begin to decompose shortly after death.

a. Biochemical oxygen demand
b. Biodegradation
c. Biofuel
d. Decomposition

4. _________ is an inorganic anion of fluorine with the chemical formula F-. It contributes no color to _________ salts. _________ is the main component of fluorite (apart from calcium ions; fluorite is roughly 49% _________ by mass), and contributes a distinctive bitter taste, but no odor to _________ salts.

a. Bifluoride
b. Bismuthide
c. Bisulfide
d. Fluoride

5. A _________ is an organic compound that contains only carbon, chlorine, and fluorine, produced as a volatile derivative of methane and ethane. They are also commonly known by the DuPont brand name Freon. The most common representative is dichlorodifluoromethane (R-12 or Freon-12).

a. Chlorofluorocarbon
b. Barra system
c. Barrier pipe
d. BE-Bridge

ANSWER KEY
6. Chemical Composition

1. d
2. a
3. d
4. d
5. a

---

7. Chemical Reactions

CHAPTER OUTLINE: KEY TERMS, PEOPLE, PLACES, CONCEPTS

- Acetic acid
- Sodium bicarbonate
- Bicarbonate
- Combustion
- Sodium
- Collision theory
- Detergent
- Dissociation
- Lewis structure
- Oxygen
- Soap scum
- Sodium carbonate
- Sodium oxide
- Hydrogen
- Precipitation
- Carbon dioxide
- Methane
- Product
- Aqueous
- Sodium chloride
- Solubility

7. Chemical Reactions

CHAPTER OUTLINE: KEY TERMS, PEOPLE, PLACES, CONCEPTS

Chloride

Silver chloride

Strong electrolyte

Spectator ion

Hydrochloric acid

Sodium hydroxide

Potassium hydroxide

Sulfuric acid

Lithium

Potassium

Gas evolution reaction

Chlorine

Redox

Straw

Electron

Natural gas

Octane

Ethanol

Bohr model

Combination reaction

Calcium carbonate

7. Chemical Reactions

CHAPTER OUTLINE: KEY TERMS, PEOPLE, PLACES, CONCEPTS

____________	Calcium oxide
____________	Calcium
____________	Decomposition
____________	Sodium nitrate
____________	Chlorofluorocarbon
____________	Ozone
____________	Dioxide

CHAPTER HIGHLIGHTS & NOTES: KEY TERMS, PEOPLE, PLACES, CONCEPTS

Acetic acid	Acetic acid is an organic compound with the chemical formula CH_3COOH (also written as CH_3CO_2H or $C_2H_4O_2$). It is a colourless liquid that when undiluted is also called glacial acetic acid. Acetic acid is the main component of vinegar (apart from water; vinegar is roughly 8% acetic acid by volume), and has a distinctive sour taste and pungent smell.
Sodium bicarbonate	Sodium bicarbonate or sodium hydrogen carbonate is the chemical compound with the formula $NaHCO_3$. Sodium bicarbonate is a white solid that is crystalline but often appears as a fine powder. It has a slightly salty, alkaline taste resembling that of washing soda (sodium carbonate).
Bicarbonate	In inorganic chemistry, bicarbonate is an intermediate form in the deprotonation of carbonic acid. It is an anion with the chemical formula HCO_3^-. Bicarbonate serves a crucial biochemical role in the physiological pH buffering system.
Combustion	Combustion or burning is the sequence of exothermic chemical reactions between a fuel and an oxidant accompanied by the production of heat and conversion of chemical species. The release of heat can produce light in the form of either glowing or a flame.

Sodium	Sodium is a chemical element with the symbol Na and atomic number 11. It is a soft, silver-white, highly reactive metal and is a member of the alkali metals; its only stable isotope is ^{23}Na. The free metal does not occur in nature, but instead must be prepared from its compounds; it was first isolated by Humphry Davy in 1807 by the electrolysis of sodium hydroxide. Sodium is the sixth most abundant element in the Earth's crust, and exists in numerous minerals such as feldspars, sodalite and rock salt.
Collision theory	Collision theory is a theory proposed independently by Max Trautz in 1916 and William Lewis in 1918, that qualitatively explains how chemical reactions occur and why reaction rates differ for different reactions. The collision theory states that when suitable particles of the reactant hit each other, only a certain percentage of the collisions cause any noticeable or significant chemical change; these successful changes are called successful collisions. The successful collisions have enough energy, also known as activation energy, at the moment of impact to break the preexisting bonds and form all new bonds.
Detergent	A detergent is a surfactant or a mixture of surfactants with 'cleaning properties in dilute solutions.' These substances are usually alkylbenzenesulfonates, a family of compounds that are similar to soap but are more soluble in hard water, because the polar sulfonate (of detergents) is less likely than the polar carboxyl to bind to calcium and other ions found in hard water. In most household contexts, the term detergent by itself refers specifically to laundry detergent or dish detergent, as opposed to hand soap or other types of cleaning agents. Detergents are commonly available as powders or concentrated solutions.
Dissociation	Dissociation in chemistry and biochemistry is a general process in which ionic compounds separate or split into smaller particles, ions, or radicals, usually in a reversible manner. For instance, when a Brønsted-Lowry acid is put in water, a covalent bond between an electronegative atom and a hydrogen atom is broken by heterolytic fission, which gives a proton and a negative ion. Dissociation is the opposite of association and recombination.
Lewis structure	Lewis structures are diagrams that show the bonding between atoms of a molecule and the lone pairs of electrons that may exist in the molecule. A Lewis structure can be drawn for any covalently bonded molecule, as well as coordination compounds. The Lewis structure was named after Gilbert N
Oxygen	Oxygen is a chemical element with symbol O and atomic number 8. It is a member of the chalcogen group on the periodic table and is a highly reactive nonmetallic element and oxidizing agent that readily forms compounds (notably oxides) with most elements. By mass, oxygen is the third-most abundant element in the universe, after hydrogen and helium At STP, two atoms of the element bind to form dioxygen, a diatomic gas that is colorless, odorless, and tasteless; with the formula O2.

7. Chemical Reactions

CHAPTER HIGHLIGHTS & NOTES: KEY TERMS, PEOPLE, PLACES, CONCEPTS

Soap scum	Soap scum is an informal term for the white solid that results from the addition of soap to hard water. Hard water contains calcium or magnesium ions, which react with the fatty acid component of soap to give what are technically called lime soaps:2 $C_{17}H_{35}COO^{-}Na^{+}$ + Ca^{2+} ? $(C_{17}H_{35}COO)_2Ca$ + 2 Na^{+} In this reaction, the sodium ion in soap is replaced by calcium ions. Lime soaps are ineffective in washing dishes or clothes or hair.
Sodium carbonate	Sodium carbonate, Na_2CO_3, is a sodium salt of carbonic acid. It most commonly occurs as a crystalline heptahydrate, which readily effloresces to form a white powder, the monohydrate. Sodium carbonate is domestically well known for its everyday use as a water softener.
Sodium oxide	Sodium oxide is a chemical compound with the formula Na_2O. It is used in ceramics and glasses, though not in a raw form. Treatment with water affords sodium hydroxide. Na_2O + H_2O ? 2 NaOH The alkali metal oxides M_2O (M = Li, Na, K, Rb) crystallise in the antifluorite structure.
Hydrogen	Hydrogen is a chemical element with chemical symbol H and atomic number 1. With an atomic weight of 1.00794 u, hydrogen is the lightest element and its monatomic form (H) is the most abundant chemical substance, constituting roughly 75% of the Universe's baryonic mass. Non-remnant stars are mainly composed of hydrogen in its plasma state. At standard temperature and pressure, hydrogen is a colorless, odorless, tasteless, non-toxic, nonmetallic, highly combustible diatomic gas with the molecular formula H_2.
Precipitation	Precipitation is the formation of a solid in a solution or inside another solid during a chemical reaction or by diffusion in a solid. When the reaction occurs in a liquid solution, the solid formed is called the precipitate. The chemical that causes the solid to form is called the precipitant.
Carbon dioxide	Carbon dioxide is a naturally occurring chemical compound composed of two oxygen atoms each covalently double bonded to a single carbon atom. It is a gas at standard temperature and pressure and exists in Earth's atmosphere in this state, as a trace gas at a concentration of 0.039 per cent by volume. As part of the carbon cycle, plants, algae, and cyanobacteria use light energy to photosynthesize carbohydrate from carbon dioxide and water, with oxygen produced as a waste product.
Methane	Methane is a chemical compound with the chemical formula CH4 (one atom of carbon and four atoms of hydrogen). It is the simplest alkane and the main component of natural gas.

Product	Product are formed during chemical reactions as reagents are consumed. Products have lower energy than the reagents and are produced during the reaction according to the second law of thermodynamics. The released energy comes from changes in chemical bonds between atoms in reagent molecules and may be given off in the form of heat or light.
Aqueous	An aqueous solution is a solution in which the solvent is water. It is usually shown in chemical equations by appending (aq) to the relevant formula. For example, a solution of ordinary table salt, or sodium chloride (NaCl), in water would be represented as NaCl(aq).
Sodium chloride	Sodium chloride, also known as salt, common salt, table salt or halite, is an ionic compound with the formula NaCl, representing equal proportions of sodium and chlorine. Sodium chloride is the salt most responsible for the salinity of the ocean and of the extracellular fluid of many multicellular organisms. As the major ingredient in edible salt, it is commonly used as a condiment and food preservative.
Solubility	Solubility is the property of a solid, liquid, or gaseous chemical substance called solute to dissolve in a solid, liquid, or gaseous solvent to form a homogeneous solution of the solute in the solvent. The solubility of a substance fundamentally depends on the physical and chemical properties of the solute and solvent as well as on temperature, pressure and the pH of the solution. The extent of the solubility of a substance in a specific solvent is measured as the saturation concentration, where adding more solute does not increase the concentration of the solution and begin to precipitate the excess amount of solute.
Chloride	The chloride ion is formed when the element chlorine gains an electron to form an anion (negatively charged ion) Cl^-. The salts of hydrochloric acid contain chloride ions and can also be called chlorides. The chloride ion, and its salts such as sodium chloride, are very soluble in water.
Silver chloride	Silver chloride is a chemical compound with the chemical formula AgCl. This white crystalline solid is well known for its low solubility in water (this behavior being reminiscent of the chlorides of Tl^+ and Pb^{2+}). Upon illumination or heating, silver chloride converts to silver (and chlorine), which is signaled by greyish or purplish coloration to some samples.
Strong electrolyte	A strong electrolyte is a solute that completely, or almost completely, ionizes or dissociates in a solution. These ions are good conductors of electric current in the solution. Originally, a 'strong electrolyte' was defined as a chemical that, when in aqueous solution, is a good conductor of electricity.
Spectator ion	A spectator ion is an ion that exists as a reactant and a product in a chemical equation.

Spectator ions can, for example, be observed in the reaction of aqueous solutions of sodium chloride and copper(II) sulfate but does not affect the equilibrium:$2Na^+_{(aq)} + 2Cl^-_{(aq)} + Cu^{2+}_{(aq)} + SO_4^{2-}_{(aq)}$? $2Na^+_{(aq)} + SO_4^{2-}_{(aq)} + CuCl_{2\ (s)}$

The Na^+ and SO_4^{2-} ions are spectator ions since they remain unchanged on both sides of the equation. They simply 'watch' the other ions react, hence the name.

Hydrochloric acid

Hydrochloric acid is a clear, colorless, highly pungent solution of hydrogen chloride in water. It is a highly corrosive, strong mineral acid with many industrial uses. Hydrochloric acid is found naturally in gastric acid.

Sodium hydroxide

Sodium hydroxide, also known as caustic soda, or lye, is an inorganic compound with the chemical formula NaOH . It is a white solid, and is a highly caustic metallic base and alkali salt. It is available in pellets, flakes, granules, and as prepared solutions at a number of different concentrations.

Potassium hydroxide

Potassium hydroxide is an inorganic compound with the formula KOH, commonly called caustic potash.

Along with sodium hydroxide, this colorless solid is a prototypical strong base. It has many industrial and niche applications; most applications exploit its reactivity toward acids and its corrosive nature.

Sulfuric acid

Sulfuric acid is a highly corrosive strong mineral acid with the molecular formula H_2SO_4. It is a pungent, colorless to slightly yellow viscous liquid which is soluble in water at all concentrations. Sometimes, it is dyed dark brown during production to alert people to its hazards.

Lithium

Lithium is a chemical element with symbol Li and atomic number 3. It is a soft, silver-white metal belonging to the alkali metal group of chemical elements. Under standard conditions it is the lightest metal and the least dense solid element. Like all alkali metals, lithium is highly reactive and flammable.

Potassium

Potassium is a chemical element with symbol K and atomic number 19. Elemental potassium is a soft silvery-white alkali metal that oxidizes rapidly in air and is very reactive with water, generating sufficient heat to ignite the hydrogen emitted in the reaction and burning with a lilac flame.

Because potassium and sodium are chemically very similar, their salts were not at first differentiated. The existence of multiple elements in their salts was suspected from 1702, and this was proven in 1807 when potassium and sodium were individually isolated from different salts by electrolysis.

7. Chemical Reactions

Gas evolution reaction	A gas evolution reaction is a chemical reaction in which a gas, such as oxygen or carbon dioxide is produced. See also oxygen evolution.
Chlorine	Chlorine is a chemical element with symbol Cl and atomic number 17. Chlorine is in the halogen group (17) and is the second lightest halogen after fluorine. The element is a yellow-green gas under standard conditions, where it forms diatomic molecules. It has the highest electron affinity and the fourth highest electronegativity of all the reactive elements; for this reason, chlorine is a strong oxidizing agent.
Redox	Redox reactions include all chemical reactions in which atoms have their oxidation state changed; redox reactions generally involve the transfer of electrons between species. This can be either a simple redox process, such as the oxidation of carbon to yield carbon dioxide (CO2) or the reduction of carbon by hydrogen to yield methane (CH_4), or a complex process such as the oxidation of glucose ($C_6H_{12}O_6$) in the human body through a series of complex electron transfer processes. The term 'redox' comes from two concepts involved with electron transfer: reduction and oxidation.
Straw	Straw is an agricultural by-product, the dry stalks of cereal plants, after the grain and chaff have been removed. Straw makes up about half of the yield of cereal crops such as barley, oats, rice, rye and wheat. It has many uses, including fuel, livestock bedding and fodder, thatching and basket -making.
Electron	The electron is a subatomic particle with a negative elementary electric charge. Electrons belong to the first generation of the lepton particle family, and are generally thought to be elementary particles because they have no known components or substructure. The electron has a mass that is approximately 1/1836 that of the proton.
Natural gas	Natural gas is a fossil fuel formed when layers of buried plants and animals are exposed to intense heat and pressure over thousands of years. The energy that the plants originally obtained from the sun is stored in the form of carbon in natural gas. Natural gas is a nonrenewable resource because it cannot be replenished on a human time frame.
Octane	Octane is a hydrocarbon and an alkane with the chemical formula C_8H_{18}, and the condensed structural formula $CH_{36}CH_3$. Octane has many structural isomers that differ by the amount and location of branching in the carbon chain. One of these isomers, 2,2,4-trimethylpentane (isooctane) is used as one of the standard values in the octane rating scale.
Ethanol	Ethanol, also called ethyl alcohol, pure alcohol, grain alcohol, or drinking alcohol, is a volatile, flammable, colorless liquid with the structural formula CH_3CH_2OH, often abbreviated as C_2H_5OH or C_2H_6O.

7. Chemical Reactions

A psychoactive drug and one of the oldest recreational drugs, ethanol can cause alcohol intoxication when consumed. Best known as the type of alcohol found in alcoholic beverages, it is also used in thermometers, as a solvent, and as a fuel. In common usage, it is often referred to simply as alcohol or spirits.

Bohr model

In atomic physics, the Bohr model, introduced by Niels Bohr in 1913, depicts the atom as small, positively charged nucleus surrounded by electrons that travel in circular orbits around the nucleus--similar in structure to the solar system, but with attraction provided by electrostatic forces rather than gravity. After the cubic model .•Quantum ruleThe angular momentum L = $m_e vr$ is an integer multiple of h: $m_e vr = n\hbar$ Substituting the expression for the velocity gives an equation for r in terms of n: $\sqrt{Zk_e e^2 m_e r} = n\hbar$ so that the allowed orbit radius at any n is: $r_n = \frac{n^2\hbar^2}{Zk_e e^2 m_e}$ The smallest possible value of r in the hydrogen atom is called the Bohr radius and is equal to: $r_1 = \frac{\hbar^2}{k_e e^2 m_e} \approx 5.29 \times 10^{-11} \mathrm{m}$ The energy of the n-th level for any atom is determined by the radius and quantum number:

$$E = -\frac{Zk_e e^2}{2r_n} = -\frac{Z^2(k_e e^2)^2 m_e}{2\hbar^2 n^2} \approx \frac{-13.6Z^2}{n^2}\mathrm{eV}$$

An electron in the lowest energy level of hydrogen therefore has about 13.6 eV less energy than a motionless electron infinitely far from the nucleus. The next energy level is -3.4 eV. The third (n = 3) is -1.51 eV, and so on.

Combination reaction

Those reaction in which two or more elements or compounds combine together to form a single compound are called combination reaction. They may be represented by X + Y ? XY Combination reactions are usually exothermic. For example barium metal and fluorine gas will combine in a highly exothermic reaction to form the salt barium fluoride:

Ba + F_2?BaF_2

Another example is magnesium oxide combining with carbon dioxide to produce magnesium carbonate.

Calcium carbonate

Calcium carbonate is a chemical compound with the formula $CaCO_3$. It is a common substance found in rocks in all parts of the world, and is the main component of shells of marine organisms, snails, coal balls, pearls, and eggshells. Calcium carbonate is the active ingredient in agricultural lime, and is created when Ca ions in hard water react with carbonate ions creating limescale.

Calcium oxide

Calcium oxide, commonly known as quicklime or burnt lime, is a widely used chemical compound. It is a white, caustic, alkaline crystalline solid at room temperature. The broadly used term 'lime' connotes calcium-containing inorganic materials, which include carbonates, oxides and hydroxides of calcium, silicon, magnesium, aluminium, and iron predominate, such as limestone.

Calcium

Calcium is the chemical element with symbol Ca and atomic number 20. Calcium is a soft gray alkaline earth metal, and is the fifth-most-abundant element by mass in the Earth's crust. Calcium is also the fifth-most-abundant dissolved ion in seawater by both molarity and mass, after sodium, chloride, magnesium, and sulfate.

Calcium is essential for living organisms, in particular in cell physiology, where movement of the calcium ion Ca^{2+} into and out of the cytoplasm functions as a signal for many cellular processes.

Decomposition

Decomposition is the process by which organic substances are broken down into simpler forms of matter. The process is essential for recycling the finite matter that occupies physical space in the biome. Bodies of living organisms begin to decompose shortly after death.

Sodium nitrate

Sodium nitrate is the chemical compound with the formula $NaNO_3$. This salt is also known as Chile saltpeter or Peru saltpeter (due to the large deposits found in each country) to distinguish it from ordinary saltpeter, potassium nitrate. The mineral form is also known as nitratine, nitratite or soda niter.

Chlorofluorocarbon

A chlorofluorocarbon is an organic compound that contains only carbon, chlorine, and fluorine, produced as a volatile derivative of methane and ethane. They are also commonly known by the DuPont brand name Freon. The most common representative is dichlorodifluoromethane (R-12 or Freon-12).

Ozone

Ozone, or trioxygen, is an inorganic compound with the chemical formula O3(μ-O) (also written [O (μ-O)O] or O3). It is a pale blue gas with a distinctively pungent smell. It is an allotrope of oxygen that is much less stable than the diatomic allotrope O2, breaking down in the lower atmosphere to normal dioxygen.

Dioxide

An oxide is a chemical compound that contains at least one oxygen atom and one other element in its chemical formula. Metal oxides typically contain an anion of oxygen in the oxidation state of -2. Most of the Earth's crust consists of solid oxides, the result of elements being oxidized by the oxygen in air or in water. Hydrocarbon combustion affords the two principal carbon oxides: carbon monoxide and carbon dioxide.

7. Chemical Reactions

CHAPTER QUIZ: KEY TERMS, PEOPLE, PLACES, CONCEPTS

1. _________ or sodium hydrogen carbonate is the chemical compound with the formula $NaHCO_3$. _________ is a white solid that is crystalline but often appears as a fine powder. It has a slightly salty, alkaline taste resembling that of washing soda (sodium carbonate).

   a. Sodium bicarbonate
   b. Base modifying agent
   c. Calcium oxide
   d. Free base

2. _________ is a chemical element with symbol O and atomic number 8. It is a member of the chalcogen group on the periodic table and is a highly reactive nonmetallic element and oxidizing agent that readily forms compounds (notably oxides) with most elements. By mass, _________ is the third-most abundant element in the universe, after hydrogen and helium At STP, two atoms of the element bind to form di_________, a diatomic gas that is colorless, odorless, and tasteless; with the formula O2.

   Many major classes of organic molecules in living organisms, such as proteins, nucleic acids, carbohydrates, and fats, contain _________, as do the major inorganic compounds that are constituents of animal shells, teeth, and bone.

   a. Oxygen
   b. Berkelium
   c. Beryllium
   d. Bismuth

3. _________ is an organic compound with the chemical formula CH_3COOH (also written as CH_3CO_2H or $C_2H_4O_2$). It is a colourless liquid that when undiluted is also called glacial _________. _________ is the main component of vinegar (apart from water; vinegar is roughly 8% _________ by volume), and has a distinctive sour taste and pungent smell.

   a. Bisulfide
   b. Buffering agent
   c. Carbonate alkalinity
   d. Acetic acid

4. _________ is a chemical compound with the formula Na_2O. It is used in ceramics and glasses, though not in a raw form. Treatment with water affords sodium hydroxide. $Na_2O + H_2O$? 2 NaOH

   The alkali metal oxides M_2O (M = Li, Na, K, Rb) crystallise in the antifluorite structure.

   a. Sodium oxide
   b. Boron trioxide
   c. Calcium oxide
   d. Lanthanum oxide

5. _________ or burning is the sequence of exothermic chemical reactions between a fuel and an oxidant accompanied by the production of heat and conversion of chemical species. The release of heat can produce light in the form of either glowing or a flame.

   In a complete _________ reaction, a compound reacts with an oxidizing element, such as oxygen or fluorine, and the products are compounds of each element in the fuel with the oxidizing element.

   a. Chalcogel
   b. Combustion
   c. Ceration
   d. Congelation

ANSWER KEY
7. Chemical Reactions

---

1. a
2. a
3. d
4. a
5. b

---

8. Quantities in Chemical Reactions

CHAPTER OUTLINE: KEY TERMS, PEOPLE, PLACES, CONCEPTS

- Carbon dioxide
- Fossil fuel
- Octane
- Combustion
- Dioxide
- Greenhouse gas
- Stoichiometry
- Lewis structure
- Nitrite
- Hydrogen
- Mole
- Nitrogen
- Product
- Carbon monoxide
- Ethanol
- Titanium
- Endothermic
- Enthalpy
- Excited state
- Methane
- Natural gas

8. Quantities in Chemical Reactions

CHAPTER OUTLINE: KEY TERMS, PEOPLE, PLACES, CONCEPTS

	Oxygen
	Thermal energy
	Propane

CHAPTER HIGHLIGHTS & NOTES: KEY TERMS, PEOPLE, PLACES, CONCEPTS

Carbon dioxide

Carbon dioxide is a naturally occurring chemical compound composed of two oxygen atoms each covalently double bonded to a single carbon atom. It is a gas at standard temperature and pressure and exists in Earth's atmosphere in this state, as a trace gas at a concentration of 0.039 per cent by volume.

As part of the carbon cycle, plants, algae, and cyanobacteria use light energy to photosynthesize carbohydrate from carbon dioxide and water, with oxygen produced as a waste product.

Fossil fuel

Fossil fuels are fuels formed by natural processes such as anaerobic decomposition of buried dead organisms. The age of the organisms and their resulting fossil fuels is typically millions of years, and sometimes exceeds 650 million years. Fossil fuels contain high percentages of carbon and include coal, petroleum, and natural gas.

Octane

Octane is a hydrocarbon and an alkane with the chemical formula C_8H_{18}, and the condensed structural formula $CH_{36}CH_3$. Octane has many structural isomers that differ by the amount and location of branching in the carbon chain. One of these isomers, 2,2,4-trimethylpentane (isooctane) is used as one of the standard values in the octane rating scale.

Combustion

Combustion or burning is the sequence of exothermic chemical reactions between a fuel and an oxidant accompanied by the production of heat and conversion of chemical species. The release of heat can produce light in the form of either glowing or a flame.

In a complete combustion reaction, a compound reacts with an oxidizing element, such as oxygen or fluorine, and the products are compounds of each element in the fuel with the oxidizing element.

Dioxide

An oxide is a chemical compound that contains at least one oxygen atom and one other element in its chemical formula. Metal oxides typically contain an anion of oxygen in the oxidation state of -2.

8. Quantities in Chemical Reactions

Most of the Earth's crust consists of solid oxides, the result of elements being oxidized by the oxygen in air or in water. Hydrocarbon combustion affords the two principal carbon oxides: carbon monoxide and carbon dioxide.

Greenhouse gas

A greenhouse gas is a gas in an atmosphere that absorbs and emits radiation within the thermal infrared range. This process is the fundamental cause of the greenhouse effect. The primary greenhouse gases in the Earth's atmosphere are water vapor, carbon dioxide methane, nitrous oxide, and ozone.

Stoichiometry

Stoichiometry is a branch of chemistry that deals with the relative quantities of reactants and products in chemical reactions. In a balanced chemical reaction, the relations among quantities of reactants and products typically form a ratio of positive integers. For example, in a reaction that forms ammonia (NH_3), exactly one molecule of nitrogen gas (N_2) reacts with three molecules of hydrogen gas (H_2) to produce two molecules of NH_3:N2 + 3H2 ? 2NH3

This particular kind of stoichiometry - describing the quantitative relationships among substances as they participate in chemical reactions - is known as reaction stoichiometry.

Lewis structure

Lewis structures are diagrams that show the bonding between atoms of a molecule and the lone pairs of electrons that may exist in the molecule. A Lewis structure can be drawn for any covalently bonded molecule, as well as coordination compounds. The Lewis structure was named after Gilbert N

Nitrite

The nitrite ion, which has the chemical formula NO_2^-, is a symmetric anion with equal N-O bond lengths and an O-N-O bond angle of approximately 120°. Upon protonation, the unstable weak acid nitrous acid is produced. Nitrite can be oxidized or reduced, with the product somewhat dependent on the oxidizing/reducing agent and its strength.

Hydrogen

Hydrogen is a chemical element with chemical symbol H and atomic number 1. With an atomic weight of 1.00794 u, hydrogen is the lightest element and its monatomic form (H) is the most abundant chemical substance, constituting roughly 75% of the Universe's baryonic mass. Non-remnant stars are mainly composed of hydrogen in its plasma state.

At standard temperature and pressure, hydrogen is a colorless, odorless, tasteless, non-toxic, nonmetallic, highly combustible diatomic gas with the molecular formula H_2.

Mole

Mole is a unit of measurement used in chemistry to express amounts of a chemical substance, defined as the amount of any substance that contains as many elementary entities (e.g., atoms, molecules, ions, electrons) as there are atoms in 12 grams of pure carbon-12, the isotope of carbon with relative atomic mass 12. This corresponds to the Avogadro constant, which has a value of $6.02214129(27)\times10^{23}$ elementary entities of the substance.

8. Quantities in Chemical Reactions

It is one of the base units in the International System of Units, and has the unit symbol mol and corresponds with the dimension symbol N. In honour of the unit, chemists often celebrate October 23 (a reference to the 10^{23} part of Avogadro's number) as 'Mole Day'.

The mole is widely used in chemistry instead of units of mass or volume as a convenient way to express amounts of reactants or of products of chemical reactions.

Nitrogen

Nitrogen, symbol N, is the chemical element of atomic number 7. At room temperature, it is a gas of diatomic molecules and is colorless and odorless. Nitrogen is a common element in the universe, estimated at about seventh in total abundance in our galaxy and the Solar System. On Earth, the element is primarily found as the free element; it forms about 80% of the Earth's atmosphere.

Product

Product are formed during chemical reactions as reagents are consumed. Products have lower energy than the reagents and are produced during the reaction according to the second law of thermodynamics. The released energy comes from changes in chemical bonds between atoms in reagent molecules and may be given off in the form of heat or light.

Carbon monoxide

Carbon monoxide is a colorless, odorless, and tasteless gas that is slightly less dense than air. It is toxic to humans and animals when encountered in higher concentrations, although it is also produced in normal animal metabolism in low quantities, and is thought to have some normal biological functions. In the atmosphere, it is spatially variable, short lived, having a role in the formation of ground-level ozone.

Ethanol

Ethanol, also called ethyl alcohol, pure alcohol, grain alcohol, or drinking alcohol, is a volatile, flammable, colorless liquid with the structural formula CH_3CH_2OH, often abbreviated as C_2H_5OH or C_2H_6O. A psychoactive drug and one of the oldest recreational drugs, ethanol can cause alcohol intoxication when consumed. Best known as the type of alcohol found in alcoholic beverages, it is also used in thermometers, as a solvent, and as a fuel. In common usage, it is often referred to simply as alcohol or spirits.

Titanium

Titanium is a chemical element with the symbol Ti and atomic number 22. It is a lustrous transition metal with a silver color, low density and high strength. It is highly resistant to corrosion in sea water, aqua regia and chlorine.

Titanium was discovered in Cornwall, Great Britain, by William Gregor in 1791 and named by Martin Heinrich Klaproth for the Titans of Greek mythology.

Endothermic

In thermodynamics, the term endothermic describes a process or reaction in which the system absorbs energy from its surroundings in the form of heat. It is a modern coinage from Greek roots.

Enthalpy

Enthalpy is a measure of the total energy of a thermodynamic system. It includes the system's internal energy and thermodynamic potential (a state function), as well as its volume and pressure (the energy required to 'make room for it' by displacing its environment, which is an extensive quantity). The unit of measurement for enthalpy in the International System of Units (SI) is the joule, but other historical, conventional units are still in use, such as the British thermal unit and the calorie.

Excited state

Excitation is an elevation in energy level above an arbitrary baseline energy state. In physics there is a specific technical definition for energy level which is often associated with an atom being excited to an excited state.

In quantum mechanics an excited state of a system (such as an atom, molecule or nucleus) is any quantum state of the system that has a higher energy than the ground state (that is, more energy than the absolute minimum).

Methane

Methane is a chemical compound with the chemical formula CH4 (one atom of carbon and four atoms of hydrogen). It is the simplest alkane and the main component of natural gas. The relative abundance of methane makes it an attractive fuel.

Natural gas

Natural gas is a fossil fuel formed when layers of buried plants and animals are exposed to intense heat and pressure over thousands of years. The energy that the plants originally obtained from the sun is stored in the form of carbon in natural gas. Natural gas is a nonrenewable resource because it cannot be replenished on a human time frame.

Oxygen

Oxygen is a chemical element with symbol O and atomic number 8. It is a member of the chalcogen group on the periodic table and is a highly reactive nonmetallic element and oxidizing agent that readily forms compounds (notably oxides) with most elements. By mass, oxygen is the third-most abundant element in the universe, after hydrogen and helium At STP, two atoms of the element bind to form dioxygen, a diatomic gas that is colorless, odorless, and tasteless; with the formula O2.

Many major classes of organic molecules in living organisms, such as proteins, nucleic acids, carbohydrates, and fats, contain oxygen, as do the major inorganic compounds that are constituents of animal shells, teeth, and bone.

Thermal energy

Thermal energy is the part of the total potential energy and kinetic energy of an object or sample of matter that results in the system temperature. It is represented by the variable Q, and can be measured in Joules. This quantity may be difficult to determine or even meaningless unless the system has attained its temperature only through warming (heating), and not been subjected to work input or output, or any other energy-changing processes.

Propane

Propane is a three-carbon alkane with the molecular formula C3H

8. Quantities in Chemical Reactions

CHAPTER HIGHLIGHTS & NOTES: KEY TERMS, PEOPLE, PLACES, CONCEPTS

8, normally a gas, but compressible to a transportable liquid. A by-product of natural gas processing and petroleum refining, it is commonly used as a fuel for engines, oxy-gas torches, barbecues, portable stoves, and residential central heating. Propane is one of a group of liquefied petroleum gases.

CHAPTER QUIZ: KEY TERMS, PEOPLE, PLACES, CONCEPTS

1. _________s are fuels formed by natural processes such as anaerobic decomposition of buried dead organisms. The age of the organisms and their resulting _________s is typically millions of years, and sometimes exceeds 650 million years. _________s contain high percentages of carbon and include coal, petroleum, and natural gas.

a. Binary acid
b. Carbonic acid
c. Chiral Lewis acid
d. Fossil fuel

2. _________ is a naturally occurring chemical compound composed of two oxygen atoms each covalently double bonded to a single carbon atom. It is a gas at standard temperature and pressure and exists in Earth's atmosphere in this state, as a trace gas at a concentration of 0.039 per cent by volume.

As part of the carbon cycle, plants, algae, and cyanobacteria use light energy to photosynthesize carbohydrate from _________ and water, with oxygen produced as a waste product.

a. Barium acetylacetonate
b. Cerium acetylacetonate
c. Dysprosium acetylacetonate
d. Carbon dioxide

3. In thermodynamics, the term _________ describes a process or reaction in which the system absorbs energy from its surroundings in the form of heat. It is a modern coinage from Greek roots. The prefix endo- derives from the Greek word 'endon' (??d??) meaning 'within,' and the latter part of the word comes from the Greek word root 'therm' (?e?µ-) meaning 'hot.' The intended sense is that of a reaction that depends on taking in heat if it is to proceed.

a. Calorimeter constant
b. Ceiling temperature
c. Endothermic
d. Chalcogel

4. . _________ or burning is the sequence of exothermic chemical reactions between a fuel and an oxidant accompanied by the production of heat and conversion of chemical species.

The release of heat can produce light in the form of either glowing or a flame.

In a complete _________ reaction, a compound reacts with an oxidizing element, such as oxygen or fluorine, and the products are compounds of each element in the fuel with the oxidizing element.

a. Chalcogel
b. SEAgel
c. Ceration
d. Combustion

5. A _________ is a gas in an atmosphere that absorbs and emits radiation within the thermal infrared range. This process is the fundamental cause of the greenhouse effect. The primary _________es in the Earth's atmosphere are water vapor, carbon dioxide, methane, nitrous oxide, and ozone.

a. Bisulfide
b. Buffer solution
c. Buffering agent
d. Greenhouse gas

ANSWER KEY
8. Quantities in Chemical Reactions

---

1. d
2. d
3. c
4. d
5. d

---

9. Electrons in Atoms and the Periodic Table

CHAPTER OUTLINE: KEY TERMS, PEOPLE, PLACES, CONCEPTS

- Electron
- Lewis structure
- Helium
- Hydrogen
- Algebra
- Alkali metal
- Bohr model
- Einstein
- Electromagnetic radiation
- Fluorine
- Alkali
- Neutron
- Proton
- Collision theory
- Frequency
- Electromagnetic spectrum
- Photon
- Atom
- Continuous spectrum
- Emission spectrum
- Quantum

9. Electrons in Atoms and the Periodic Table

CHAPTER OUTLINE: KEY TERMS, PEOPLE, PLACES, CONCEPTS

Ground state

Principal quantum number

Excited state

Electron configuration

Pauli exclusion

Pauli exclusion principle

Lithium

Straw

Core electron

Periodic table

Silicon

Valence electron

Chloride ion

Phosphorus

Ionization energy

Ionization

9. Electrons in Atoms and the Periodic Table

CHAPTER HIGHLIGHTS & NOTES: KEY TERMS, PEOPLE, PLACES, CONCEPTS

Electron	The electron is a subatomic particle with a negative elementary electric charge. Electrons belong to the first generation of the lepton particle family, and are generally thought to be elementary particles because they have no known components or substructure. The electron has a mass that is approximately 1/1836 that of the proton.
Lewis structure	Lewis structures are diagrams that show the bonding between atoms of a molecule and the lone pairs of electrons that may exist in the molecule. A Lewis structure can be drawn for any covalently bonded molecule, as well as coordination compounds. The Lewis structure was named after Gilbert N
Helium	Helium is a chemical element with symbol He and atomic number 2. It is a colorless, odorless, tasteless, non-toxic, inert, monatomic gas that heads the noble gas group in the periodic table. Its boiling and melting points are the lowest among the elements and it exists only as a gas except in extreme conditions. Helium is the second lightest element and is the second most abundant element in the observable universe, being present at about 24% of the total elemental mass, which is more than 12 times the mass of all the heavier elements combined.
Hydrogen	Hydrogen is a chemical element with chemical symbol H and atomic number 1. With an atomic weight of 1.00794 u, hydrogen is the lightest element and its monatomic form (H) is the most abundant chemical substance, constituting roughly 75% of the Universe's baryonic mass. Non-remnant stars are mainly composed of hydrogen in its plasma state. At standard temperature and pressure, hydrogen is a colorless, odorless, tasteless, non-toxic, nonmetallic, highly combustible diatomic gas with the molecular formula H_2.
Algebra	Algebra is one of the broad parts of mathematics, together with number theory, geometry and analysis. As such, it includes everything from elementary equation solving to the study of abstractions such as groups, rings, and fields. The more basic parts of algebra are called elementary algebra, the more abstract parts are called abstract algebra or modern algebra.
Alkali metal	The alkali metals are a group in the periodic table consisting of the chemical elements lithium, sodium (Na), potassium (K), rubidium (Rb), caesium (Cs), and francium (Fr). This group lies in the s-block of the periodic table as all alkali metals have their outermost electron in an s-orbital. The alkali metals provide the best example of group trends in properties in the periodic table, with elements exhibiting well-characterized homologous behaviour.
Bohr model	In atomic physics, the Bohr model, introduced by Niels Bohr in 1913, depicts the atom as small, positively charged nucleus surrounded by electrons that travel in circular orbits around the nucleus--similar in structure to the solar system, but with attraction provided by electrostatic forces rather than gravity. After the cubic model .•Quantum ruleThe angular momentum

L = $m_e$vr is an integer multiple of h: $m_e vr = n\hbar$ Substituting the expression for the velocity gives an equation for r in terms of n: $\sqrt{Zk_e e^2 m_e r} = n\hbar$ so that the allowed orbit radius at any n is: $r_n = \frac{n^2\hbar^2}{Zk_e e^2 m_e}$ The smallest possible value of r in the hydrogen atom is called the Bohr radius and is equal to: $r_1 = \frac{\hbar^2}{k_e e^2 m_e} \approx 5.29 \times 10^{-11}\mathrm{m}$ The energy of the n-th level for any atom is determined by the radius and quantum number: $E = -\frac{Zk_e e^2}{2r_n} = -\frac{Z^2(k_e e^2)^2 m_e}{2\hbar^2 n^2} \approx \frac{-13.6Z^2}{n^2}\mathrm{eV}$

An electron in the lowest energy level of hydrogen therefore has about 13.6 eV less energy than a motionless electron infinitely far from the nucleus. The next energy level is -3.4 eV. The third (n = 3) is -1.51 eV, and so on.

Einstein

An einstein is a unit defined as the energy in one mole of photons. Because energy is inversely proportional to wavelength, the unit is frequency dependent. This unit is not part of the International System of Units and is redundant with the joule.

Electromagnetic radiation

Electromagnetic radiation is one of the fundamental phenomena of electromagnetism, behaving as waves propagating through space, and also as photon particles traveling through space, carrying radiant energy. In a vacuum, it propagates at a characteristic speed, the speed of light, normally in straight lines. EMR is emitted and absorbed by charged particles.

Fluorine

Fluorine is the chemical element with symbol F and atomic number 9. At room temperature, the element is a pale yellow gas composed of diatomic molecules, F2. Fluorine is the lightest halogen and the most electronegative element. It requires great care in handling as it is extremely reactive and poisonous.

Alkali

In chemistry, an alkali is a basic, ionic salt of an alkali metal or alkaline earth metal chemical element. Some authors also define an alkali as a base that dissolves in water. A solution of a soluble base has a pH greater than 7.0. The adjective alkaline is commonly, and alkalescent less often, used in English as a synonym for basic, especially for soluble bases.

Neutron

The neutron is a subatomic hadron particle that has the symbol n or n0, no net electric charge and a mass slightly larger than that of a proton. With the exception of hydrogen-1, nuclei of atoms consist of protons and neutrons, which are therefore collectively referred to as nucleons. The number of protons in a nucleus is the atomic number and defines the type of element the atom forms.

9. Electrons in Atoms and the Periodic Table

CHAPTER HIGHLIGHTS & NOTES: KEY TERMS, PEOPLE, PLACES, CONCEPTS

Proton	The proton is a subatomic particle with the symbol p or p+ and a positive electric charge of 1 elementary charge. One or more protons are present in the nucleus of each atom. The number of protons in each atom is its atomic number.
Collision theory	Collision theory is a theory proposed independently by Max Trautz in 1916 and William Lewis in 1918, that qualitatively explains how chemical reactions occur and why reaction rates differ for different reactions. The collision theory states that when suitable particles of the reactant hit each other, only a certain percentage of the collisions cause any noticeable or significant chemical change; these successful changes are called successful collisions. The successful collisions have enough energy, also known as activation energy, at the moment of impact to break the preexisting bonds and form all new bonds.
Frequency	Frequency is the number of occurrences of a repeating event per unit time. It is also referred to as temporal frequency, which emphasizes the contrast to spatial frequency and angular frequency. The period is the duration of one cycle in a repeating event, so the period is the reciprocal of the frequency.
Electromagnetic spectrum	The electromagnetic spectrum is the range of all possible frequencies of electromagnetic radiation. The 'electromagnetic spectrum' of an object has a different meaning, and is instead the characteristic distribution of electromagnetic radiation emitted or absorbed by that particular object. The electromagnetic spectrum extends from below the low frequencies used for modern radio communication to gamma radiation at the short-wavelength (high-frequency) end, thereby covering wavelengths from thousands of kilometers down to a fraction of the size of an atom.
Photon	A photon is an elementary particle, the quantum of light and all other forms of electromagnetic radiation, and the force carrier for the electromagnetic force, even when static via virtual photons. The effects of this force are easily observable at both the microscopic and macroscopic level, because the photon has zero rest mass; this allows long distance interactions. Like all elementary particles, photons are currently best explained by quantum mechanics and exhibit wave-particle duality, exhibiting properties of both waves and particles.
Atom	The atom is a basic unit of matter that consists of a dense central nucleus surrounded by a cloud of negatively charged electrons. The atomic nucleus contains a mix of positively charged protons and electrically neutral neutrons, which means 'uncuttable' or 'the smallest indivisible particle of matter'. Although the Indian and Greek concepts of the atom were based purely on philosophy, modern science has retained the name coined by Democritus.
Continuous spectrum	In physics, a continuous spectrum usually means a set of values for some physical quantity that is best described as an interval of real numbers. It is opposed to discrete spectrum, a set of values that is discrete in the mathematical sense, where there is a positive gap between each value and the next one.

Emission spectrum

The emission spectrum of a chemical element or chemical compound is the spectrum of frequencies of electromagnetic radiation emitted due to an atom's electrons making a transition from a high energy state to a lower energy state. The energy of the emitted photon is equal to the energy difference between the two states. There are many possible electron transitions for each atom, and each transition has a specific energy difference.

Quantum

In physics, a quantum is the minimum amount of any physical entity involved in an interaction. Behind this, one finds the fundamental notion that a physical property may be 'quantized,' referred to as 'the hypothesis of quantization'. This means that the magnitude can take on only certain discrete values.

Ground state

The ground state of a quantum mechanical system is its lowest-energy state; the energy of the ground state is known as the zero-point energy of the system. An excited state is any state with energy greater than the ground state. The ground state of a quantum field theory is usually called the vacuum state or the vacuum.

Principal quantum number

The principal quantum number, symbolized as n, is the first of a set of quantum numbers (which includes: the principal quantum number, the azimuthal quantum number, the magnetic quantum number, and the spin quantum number) of an atomic orbital. The principal quantum number can only have positive integer values. As n increases, the orbital becomes larger and the electron spends more time farther from the nucleus.

Excited state

Excitation is an elevation in energy level above an arbitrary baseline energy state. In physics there is a specific technical definition for energy level which is often associated with an atom being excited to an excited state.

In quantum mechanics an excited state of a system (such as an atom, molecule or nucleus) is any quantum state of the system that has a higher energy than the ground state (that is, more energy than the absolute minimum).

Electron configuration

In atomic physics and quantum chemistry, the electron configuration is the distribution of electrons of an atom or molecule in atomic or molecular orbitals. For example, the electron configuration of the neon atom is $1s^2\ 2s^2\ 2p^6$.

Electronic configurations describe electrons as each moving independently in an orbital, in an average field created by all other orbitals.

Pauli exclusion

The Pauli exclusion principle is the quantum mechanical principle that no two identical fermions may occupy the same quantum state simultaneously. In the case of electrons, it can be stated as follows, It is impossible for two electrons of a poly-electron atom to have the same values of the four quantum numbers (n, l, m_l and m_s). For two electrons residing in the same orbital, n, l, and m

9. Electrons in Atoms and the Periodic Table

CHAPTER HIGHLIGHTS & NOTES: KEY TERMS, PEOPLE, PLACES, CONCEPTS

Pauli exclusion principle	The Pauli exclusion principle is the quantum mechanical principle that no two identical fermions may occupy the same quantum state simultaneously. A more rigorous statement is that the total wave function for two identical fermions is anti-symmetric with respect to exchange of the particles. The principle was formulated by Austrian physicist Wolfgang Pauli in 1925.
Lithium	Lithium is a chemical element with symbol Li and atomic number 3. It is a soft, silver-white metal belonging to the alkali metal group of chemical elements. Under standard conditions it is the lightest metal and the least dense solid element. Like all alkali metals, lithium is highly reactive and flammable.
Straw	Straw is an agricultural by-product, the dry stalks of cereal plants, after the grain and chaff have been removed. Straw makes up about half of the yield of cereal crops such as barley, oats, rice, rye and wheat. It has many uses, including fuel, livestock bedding and fodder, thatching and basket -making.
Core electron	Core electrons are the electrons in an atom that are not valence electrons and therefore do not participate in bonding. An example: the carbon atom has a total of 6 electrons, 4 of them being valence electrons. So the remaining 2 electrons must be core electrons.
Periodic table	The periodic table is a tabular arrangement of the chemical elements, organized on the basis of their atomic numbers, electron configurations, and recurring chemical properties. Elements are presented in order of increasing atomic number (the number of protons in the nucleus). The standard form of the table consists of a grid of elements laid out in 18 columns and 7 rows, with a double row of elements below that.
Silicon	Silicon, a tetravalent metalloid, is a chemical element with the symbol Si and atomic number 14. It is less reactive than its chemical analog carbon, the nonmetal directly above it in the periodic table, but more reactive than germanium, the metalloid directly below it in the table. Controversy about silicon's character dates to its discovery; it was first prepared and characterized in pure form in 1823. In 1808, it was given the name silicium (from Latin: silex, hard stone or flint), with an -ium word-ending to suggest a metal, a name which the element retains in several non-English languages. However, its final English name, first suggested in 1817, reflects the more physically similar elements carbon and boron.
Valence electron	In chemistry, a valence electron is an electron that is associated with an atom, and that can participate in the formation of a chemical bond; in a single covalent bond, both atoms in the bond contribute one valence electron in order to form a shared pair. The presence of valence electrons can determine the element's chemical properties and whether it may bond with other elements: For a main group element, a valence electron can only be in the outermost electron shell. In a transition metal, a valence electron can also be in an inner shell.
Chloride ion	The chloride ion is the anion Cl^-.

It is formed when the element chlorine (a halogen) gains an electron or when a compound such as hydrogen chloride is dissolved in water or other polar solvents. Chlorides salts such as sodium chloride are often very soluble in water.

Phosphorus

Phosphorus is a nonmetallic chemical element with symbol P and atomic number 15. A multivalent pnictogen, phosphorus as a mineral is almost always present in its maximally oxidised state, as inorganic phosphate rocks. Elemental phosphorus exists in two major forms--white phosphorus and red phosphorus--but due to its high reactivity, phosphorus is never found as a free element on Earth.

The first form of elemental phosphorus to be produced (white phosphorus, in 1669) emits a faint glow upon exposure to oxygen - hence its name given from Greek mythology, F?sf???? meaning 'light-bearer' (Latin Lucifer), referring to the 'Morning Star', the planet Venus.

Ionization energy

The ionization energy of an atom or molecule describes the amount of energy required to remove an electron from the atom or molecule in the gaseous state. X + energy ? $X^+ + e^-$

The term ionization potential has been used in the past but is not recommended.

The units for ionization energy vary from discipline to discipline.

Ionization

Ionization is the process by which an atom or a molecule acquires a negative or positive charge by gaining or losing electrons.

CHAPTER QUIZ: KEY TERMS, PEOPLE, PLACES, CONCEPTS

1. _________ is an agricultural by-product, the dry stalks of cereal plants, after the grain and chaff have been removed. _________ makes up about half of the yield of cereal crops such as barley, oats, rice, rye and wheat. It has many uses, including fuel, livestock bedding and fodder, thatching and basket-making.

   a. Bubble wrap
   b. Straw
   c. Coated paper
   d. Container compression test

2. . _________ is the number of occurrences of a repeating event per unit time. It is also referred to as temporal _________, which emphasizes the contrast to spatial _________ and angular _________. The period is the duration of one cycle in a repeating event, so the period is the reciprocal of the _________.

a. Background noise
b. Bass trap
c. Frequency
d. Biophony

3. _________ is a theory proposed independently by Max Trautz in 1916 and William Lewis in 1918, that qualitatively explains how chemical reactions occur and why reaction rates differ for different reactions. The _________ states that when suitable particles of the reactant hit each other, only a certain percentage of the collisions cause any noticeable or significant chemical change; these successful changes are called successful collisions. The successful collisions have enough energy, also known as activation energy, at the moment of impact to break the preexisting bonds and form all new bonds.

a. Bioorthogonal chemistry
b. Carbonylation
c. Collision theory
d. Ceramide phosphoethanolamine synthase

4. In chemistry, a _________ is an electron that is associated with an atom, and that can participate in the formation of a chemical bond; in a single covalent bond, both atoms in the bond contribute one _________ in order to form a shared pair. The presence of _________s can determine the element's chemical properties and whether it may bond with other elements: For a main group element, a _________ can only be in the outermost electron shell. In a transition metal, a _________ can also be in an inner shell.

a. Band gap
b. Delocalized electron
c. N-electron valence state perturbation theory
d. Valence electron

5. In chemistry, an _________ is a basic, ionic salt of an _________ metal or alkaline earth metal chemical element. Some authors also define an _________ as a base that dissolves in water. A solution of a soluble base has a pH greater than 7.0. The adjective alkaline is commonly, and alkalescent less often, used in English as a synonym for basic, especially for soluble bases.

a. 18-Electron rule
b. Crucible
c. Alkali
d. Crisscross method

ANSWER KEY
9. Electrons in Atoms and the Periodic Table

---

1. b

2. c

3. c

4. d

5. c

---

10. Chemical Bonding

CHAPTER OUTLINE: KEY TERMS, PEOPLE, PLACES, CONCEPTS

Indinavir

Active site

Lewis structure

Octet rule

Covalent

Electron

Ionic bonding

Valence electron

Ionic compound

Potassium

Sulfur

Triple bond

Neutron

Proton

Polyatomic

Boron

Resonance

Ground state

Electron pair

Molecule

Ozone

10. Chemical Bonding

CHAPTER OUTLINE: KEY TERMS, PEOPLE, PLACES, CONCEPTS

______	Aspartame
______	Saccharin
______	Molecular geometry
______	Electronegativity
______	Concentration
______	Carbon
______	Carbon dioxide
______	Polar molecules

CHAPTER HIGHLIGHTS & NOTES: KEY TERMS, PEOPLE, PLACES, CONCEPTS

Indinavir	Indinavir is a protease inhibitor used as a component of highly active antiretroviral therapy (HAART) to treat HIV infection and AIDS.
Active site	In biology, the active site is the small port of an enzyme where substrate molecules bind and undergo a chemical reaction. This chemical reaction occurs when a substrate collides with and slots into the active site of an enzyme. The active site is usually found in a 3-D groove or pocket of the enzyme, lined with amino acid residues (or nucleotides in RNA enzymes).
Lewis structure	Lewis structures are diagrams that show the bonding between atoms of a molecule and the lone pairs of electrons that may exist in the molecule. A Lewis structure can be drawn for any covalently bonded molecule, as well as coordination compounds. The Lewis structure was named after Gilbert N
Octet rule	The octet rule is a chemical rule of thumb that states that atoms of low atomic number tend to combine in such a way that they each have eight electrons in their valence shells, giving them the same electronic configuration as a noble gas. The rule is applicable to the main-group elements, especially carbon, nitrogen, oxygen, and the halogens, but also to metals such as sodium or magnesium.

Covalent	A covalent bond is a chemical bond that involves the sharing of electron pairs between atoms. The stable balance of attractive and repulsive forces between atoms when they share electrons is known as covalent bonding. For many molecules, the sharing of electrons allows each atom to attain the equivalent of a full outer shell, corresponding to a stable electronic configuration.
Electron	The electron is a subatomic particle with a negative elementary electric charge. Electrons belong to the first generation of the lepton particle family, and are generally thought to be elementary particles because they have no known components or substructure. The electron has a mass that is approximately 1/1836 that of the proton.
Ionic bonding	Ionic bonding is a type of chemical bonding that involves the electrostatic attraction between oppositely charged ions. These ions represent atoms that have lost one or more electron (known as cations) and atoms that have gained one or more electrons (known as an anions). In the simplest case, the cation is a metal atom and the anion is a nonmetal atom, but these ions can be of a more complex nature, e.g. molecular ions like NH_4^+ or SO_4^{2-} It is important to recognize that pure ionic bonding - in which one atom 'steals' an electron from another - cannot exist: all ionic compounds have some degree of covalent bonding, or electron sharing.
Valence electron	In chemistry, a valence electron is an electron that is associated with an atom, and that can participate in the formation of a chemical bond; in a single covalent bond, both atoms in the bond contribute one valence electron in order to form a shared pair. The presence of valence electrons can determine the element's chemical properties and whether it may bond with other elements: For a main group element, a valence electron can only be in the outermost electron shell. In a transition metal, a valence electron can also be in an inner shell.
Ionic compound	In chemistry, an ionic compound is a chemical compound in which ions are held together in a lattice structure by ionic bonds. Usually, the positively charged portion consists of metal cations and the negatively charged portion is an anion or polyatomic ion. Ions in ionic compounds are held together by the electrostatic forces between oppositely charged bodies.
Potassium	Potassium is a chemical element with symbol K and atomic number 19. Elemental potassium is a soft silvery-white alkali metal that oxidizes rapidly in air and is very reactive with water, generating sufficient heat to ignite the hydrogen emitted in the reaction and burning with a lilac flame. Because potassium and sodium are chemically very similar, their salts were not at first differentiated. The existence of multiple elements in their salts was suspected from 1702, and this was proven in 1807 when potassium and sodium were individually isolated from different salts by electrolysis.
Sulfur	Sulfur or sulphur is a chemical element with symbol S and atomic number 16.

It is an abundant, multivalent non-metal. Under normal conditions, sulfur atoms form cyclic octatomic molecules with chemical formula S_8. Elemental sulfur is a bright yellow crystalline solid when at room temperature.

Triple bond

A triple bond in chemistry is a chemical bond between two atoms involving six bonding electrons instead of the usual two in a covalent single bond. The most common triple bond, that between two carbon atoms, can be found in alkynes. Other functional groups containing a triple bond are cyanides and isocyanides.

Neutron

The neutron is a subatomic hadron particle that has the symbol n or n0, no net electric charge and a mass slightly larger than that of a proton. With the exception of hydrogen-1, nuclei of atoms consist of protons and neutrons, which are therefore collectively referred to as nucleons. The number of protons in a nucleus is the atomic number and defines the type of element the atom forms.

Proton

The proton is a subatomic particle with the symbol p or p+ and a positive electric charge of 1 elementary charge. One or more protons are present in the nucleus of each atom. The number of protons in each atom is its atomic number.

Polyatomic

A polyatomic ion, also known as a molecular ion, is a charged chemical species composed of two or more atoms covalently bonded or of a metal complex that can be considered to be acting as a single unit. The prefix 'poly-' means 'many,' in Greek, but even ions of two atoms are commonly referred to as polyatomic. In older literature, a polyatomic ion is also referred to as a radical, and less commonly, as a radical group.

Boron

Boron is a chemical element with symbol B and atomic number 5. Because boron is produced entirely by cosmic ray spallation and not by stellar nucleosynthesis, it is a low-abundance element in both the solar system and the Earth's crust. Boron is concentrated on Earth by the water-solubility of its more common naturally occurring compounds, the borate minerals. These are mined industrially as evaporites, such as borax and kernite.

Resonance

In physics, resonance is the tendency of a system to oscillate with greater amplitude at some frequencies than at others. Frequencies at which the response amplitude is a relative maximum are known as the system's resonant frequencies, or resonance frequencies. At these frequencies, even small periodic driving forces can produce large amplitude oscillations, because the system stores vibrational energy.

Ground state

The ground state of a quantum mechanical system is its lowest-energy state; the energy of the ground state is known as the zero-point energy of the system. An excited state is any state with energy greater than the ground state. The ground state of a quantum field theory is usually called the vacuum state or the vacuum.

Electron pair	In chemistry, an electron pair consists of two electrons that occupy the same orbital but have opposite spins. The electron pair concept was introduced in a 1916 paper of Gilbert N. Lewis. Because electrons are fermions, the Pauli exclusion principle forbids these particles from having exactly the same quantum numbers.
Molecule	A molecule is an electrically neutral group of two or more atoms held together by chemical bonds. Molecules are distinguished from ions by their lack of electrical charge. However, in quantum physics, organic chemistry, and biochemistry, the term molecule is often used less strictly, also being applied to polyatomic ions.
Ozone	Ozone, or trioxygen, is an inorganic compound with the chemical formula O3(μ-O) (also written [O(μ-O)O] or O3). It is a pale blue gas with a distinctively pungent smell. It is an allotrope of oxygen that is much less stable than the diatomic allotrope O2, breaking down in the lower atmosphere to normal dioxygen.
Aspartame	Aspartame is an artificial, non-saccharide sweetener used as a sugar substitute in some foods and beverages. In the European Union, it is codified as E951. Aspartame is a methyl ester of the aspartic acid/phenylalanine dipeptide. It was first sold under the brand name NutraSweet; since 2009 it also has been sold under the brand name AminoSweet.
Saccharin	Saccharin is an artificial sweetener. The basic substance, benzoic sulfilimine, has effectively no food energy and is much sweeter than sucrose, but has a bitter or metallic aftertaste, especially at high concentrations. It is used to sweeten products such as drinks, candies, cookies, medicines, and toothpaste.
Molecular geometry	Molecular geometry is the three-dimensional arrangement of the atoms that constitute a molecule. It determines several properties of a substance including its reactivity, polarity, phase of matter, color, magnetism, and biological activity. The angles between bonds that an atom forms depend only weakly on the rest of molecule, i.e. they can be understood as approximately local and hence transferable properties.
Electronegativity	Electronegativity, symbol ?, is a chemical property that describes the tendency of an atom or a functional group to attract electrons towards itself. An atom's electronegativity is affected by both its atomic number and the distance that its valence electrons reside from the charged nucleus. The higher the associated electronegativity number, the more an element or compound attracts electrons towards it.
Concentration	In chemistry, concentration is the abundance of a constituent divided by the total volume of a mixture. Several types of mathematical description can be distinguished: mass concentration, molar concentration, number concentration, and volume concentration.

10. Chemical Bonding

CHAPTER HIGHLIGHTS & NOTES: KEY TERMS, PEOPLE, PLACES, CONCEPTS

Carbon	Carbon fiber, alternatively graphite fiber, carbon graphite or CF, is a material consisting of fibers about 5-10 μm in diameter and composed mostly of carbon atoms. The carbon atoms are bonded together in crystals that are more or less aligned parallel to the long axis of the fiber. The crystal alignment gives the fiber high strength-to-volume ratio (making it strong for its size).
Carbon dioxide	Carbon dioxide is a naturally occurring chemical compound composed of two oxygen atoms each covalently double bonded to a single carbon atom. It is a gas at standard temperature and pressure and exists in Earth's atmosphere in this state, as a trace gas at a concentration of 0.039 per cent by volume. As part of the carbon cycle, plants, algae, and cyanobacteria use light energy to photosynthesize carbohydrate from carbon dioxide and water, with oxygen produced as a waste product.
Polar molecules	In chemistry, polarity refers to a separation of electric charge leading to a molecule or its chemical groups having an electric dipole or multipole moment. Polar molecules interact through dipole-dipole intermolecular forces and hydrogen bonds. Molecular polarity is dependent on the difference in electronegativity between atoms in a compound and the asymmetry of the compound's structure.

CHAPTER QUIZ: KEY TERMS, PEOPLE, PLACES, CONCEPTS

1. _________ or sulphur is a chemical element with symbol S and atomic number 16. It is an abundant, multivalent non-metal. Under normal conditions, _________ atoms form cyclic octatomic molecules with chemical formula S_8. Elemental _________ is a bright yellow crystalline solid when at room temperature.

   a. Baryte
   b. Berthierite
   c. Bertrandite
   d. Sulfur

2. _________ is an artificial sweetener. The basic substance, benzoic sulfilimine, has effectively no food energy and is much sweeter than sucrose, but has a bitter or metallic aftertaste, especially at high concentrations. It is used to sweeten products such as drinks, candies, cookies, medicines, and toothpaste.

   a. BAY 57-1293
   b. Benzthiazide
   c. Saccharin
   d. BRL-50481

3. _________ is a protease inhibitor used as a component of highly active antiretroviral therapy (HAART) to treat HIV infection and AIDS.

   a. 2-Acetylaminofluorene
   b. 5-Carboxamidotryptamine
   c. Indinavir
   d. Befiradol

4. A _________ bond is a chemical bond that involves the sharing of electron pairs between atoms. The stable balance of attractive and repulsive forces between atoms when they share electrons is known as _________ bonding. For many molecules, the sharing of electrons allows each atom to attain the equivalent of a full outer shell, corresponding to a stable electronic configuration.

   a. Double bond
   b. Formal charge
   c. Triple bond
   d. Covalent

5. In biology, the _________ is the small port of an enzyme where substrate molecules bind and undergo a chemical reaction. This chemical reaction occurs when a substrate collides with and slots into the _________ of an enzyme. The _________ is usually found in a 3-D groove or pocket of the enzyme, lined with amino acid residues (or nucleotides in RNA enzymes).

   a. Ceration
   b. Congelation
   c. Active site
   d. Digestion

ANSWER KEY
10. Chemical Bonding

---

1. d
2. c
3. c
4. d
5. c

---

11. Gases

CHAPTER OUTLINE: KEY TERMS, PEOPLE, PLACES, CONCEPTS

- Soap scum
- Straw
- Compressibility
- Glycolipid
- Phospholipid
- Steroid
- Atmosphere
- Millimeter of mercury
- Hand pump
- Absolute zero
- Combined gas law
- Gas law
- Avogadro
- Ideal gas
- Ideal gas law
- Argon
- Carbon dioxide
- Miscibility
- Nitrite
- Oxygen
- Dioxide

11. Gases

CHAPTER OUTLINE: KEY TERMS, PEOPLE, PLACES, CONCEPTS

- Partial pressure
- Total pressure
- Hypoxia
- Lewis structure
- Oxygen toxicity
- Vapor pressure
- Chemical reaction
- Molar volume
- Air pollution
- Carbon monoxide
- Nitrogen dioxide
- Ozone
- Sulfur dioxide

Soap scum

Soap scum is an informal term for the white solid that results from the addition of soap to hard water. Hard water contains calcium or magnesium ions, which react with the fatty acid component of soap to give what are technically called lime soaps:2 $C_{17}H_{35}COO^{-}Na^{+}$ + Ca^{2+} ? $(C_{17}H_{35}COO)_2Ca$ + 2 Na^{+}

In this reaction, the sodium ion in soap is replaced by calcium ions.

Lime soaps are ineffective in washing dishes or clothes or hair.

Straw

Straw is an agricultural by-product, the dry stalks of cereal plants, after the grain and chaff have been removed. Straw makes up about half of the yield of cereal crops such as barley, oats, rice, rye and wheat. It has many uses, including fuel, livestock bedding and fodder, thatching and basket -making.

Compressibility

In thermodynamics and fluid mechanics, compressibility is a measure of the relative volume change of a fluid or solid as a response to a pressure change.

$$\beta = -\frac{1}{V}\frac{\partial V}{\partial p}$$

where V is volume and p is pressure.

Glycolipid

Glycolipids are lipids with a carbohydrate attached. Their role is to provide energy and also serve as markers for cellular recognition.

Phospholipid

Phospholipids are a class of lipids that are a major component of all cell membranes as they can form lipid bilayers. Most phospholipids contain a diglyceride, a phosphate group, and a simple organic molecule such as choline; one exception to this rule is sphingomyelin, which is derived from sphingosine instead of glycerol. The first phospholipid identified as such in biological tissues was lecithin, or phosphatidylcholine, in the egg yolk, by Theodore Nicolas Gobley, a French chemist and pharmacist, in 1847. The structure of the phospholipid molecule generally consists of hydrophobic tails and a hydrophilic head.

Steroid

A steroid is a type of organic compound that contains a characteristic arrangement of four cycloalkane rings that are joined to each other. Examples of steroids include the dietary fat cholesterol, the sex hormones estradiol and testosterone and the anti-inflammatory drug dexamethasone.

The core of steroids is composed of twenty carbon atoms bonded together that take the form of four fused rings: three cyclohexane rings (designated as rings A, B and C in the figure to the right) and one cyclopentane ring (the D ring).

Millimeter of mercury	A millimeter of mercury is a manometric unit of pressure, formerly defined as the extra pressure generated by a column of mercury one millimetre high. It is now defined precisely as 13.5951 × 9.80665 = 133.322387415 pascals. It is denoted by the symbol 'mmHg'.
Hand pump	Hand pumps are manually operated pumps; they use human power and mechanical advantage to move fluids or air from one place to another. They are widely used in every country in the world for a variety of industrial, marine, irrigation and leisure activities. There are many different types of hand pump available, mainly operating on a piston, diaphragm or rotary vane principle with a check valve on the entry and exit ports to the chamber operating in opposing directions.
Absolute zero	Absolute zero is the lowest temperature possible. More formally, it is the temperature at which entropy reaches its minimum value. The laws of thermodynamics state that absolute zero cannot be reached using only thermodynamic means.
Combined gas law	The combined gas law is a gas law which combines Charles's law, Boyle's law, and Gay-Lussac's law. There is no official founder for this law; it is merely an amalgamation of the three previously discovered laws. These laws each relate one thermodynamic variable to another mathematically while holding everything else constant.
Gas law	The early gas laws were developed at the end of the 18th century, when scientists began to realize that relationships between the pressure, volume and temperature of a sample of gas could be obtained which would hold for all gases. Gases behave in a similar way over a wide variety of conditions because to a good approximation they all have molecules which are widely spaced, and nowadays the equation of state for an ideal gas is derived from kinetic theory. The earlier gas laws are now considered as special cases of the ideal gas equation, with one or more of the variables held constant.
Avogadro	Avogadro is a molecular editor designed for cross-platform use in computational chemistry, molecular modeling, bioinformatics, materials science, and related areas. It is extensible through a plugin architecture.
Ideal gas	An ideal gas is a theoretical gas composed of a set of randomly moving, non-interacting point particles. The ideal gas concept is useful because it obeys the ideal gas law, a simplified equation of state, and is amenable to analysis under statistical mechanics. At normal conditions such as standard temperature and pressure, most real gases behave qualitatively like an ideal gas.
Ideal gas law	The ideal gas law is the equation of state of a hypothetical ideal gas. It is a good approximation to the behaviour of many gases under many conditions, although it has several limitations. It was first stated by Émile Clapeyron in 1834 as a combination of Boyle's law and Charles's law.
Argon	Argon is a chemical element with symbol Ar and atomic number 18.

It is in group 18 of the periodic table and is a noble gas. Argon is the third most common gas in the Earth's atmosphere, at 0.93% (9,300 ppm), making it approximately 23.8 times as abundant as the next most common atmospheric gas, carbon dioxide (390 ppm), and more than 500 times as abundant as the next most common noble gas, neon (18 ppm). Nearly all of this argon is radiogenic argon-40 derived from the decay of potassium-40 in the Earth's crust.

Carbon dioxide

Carbon dioxide is a naturally occurring chemical compound composed of two oxygen atoms each covalently double bonded to a single carbon atom. It is a gas at standard temperature and pressure and exists in Earth's atmosphere in this state, as a trace gas at a concentration of 0.039 per cent by volume.

As part of the carbon cycle, plants, algae, and cyanobacteria use light energy to photosynthesize carbohydrate from carbon dioxide and water, with oxygen produced as a waste product.

Miscibility

Miscibility is the property of substances to mix in all proportions, forming a homogeneous solution. The term is most often used to refer to liquids, but applies also to solids and gases. Water and ethanol, for example, are miscible because they mix in all proportions.

Nitrite

The nitrite ion, which has the chemical formula NO_2^-, is a symmetric anion with equal N-O bond lengths and an O-N-O bond angle of approximately 120°. Upon protonation, the unstable weak acid nitrous acid is produced. Nitrite can be oxidized or reduced, with the product somewhat dependent on the oxidizing/reducing agent and its strength.

Oxygen

Oxygen is a chemical element with symbol O and atomic number 8. It is a member of the chalcogen group on the periodic table and is a highly reactive nonmetallic element and oxidizing agent that readily forms compounds (notably oxides) with most elements. By mass, oxygen is the third-most abundant element in the universe, after hydrogen and helium At STP, two atoms of the element bind to form dioxygen, a diatomic gas that is colorless, odorless, and tasteless; with the formula O2.

Many major classes of organic molecules in living organisms, such as proteins, nucleic acids, carbohydrates, and fats, contain oxygen, as do the major inorganic compounds that are constituents of animal shells, teeth, and bone.

Dioxide

An oxide is a chemical compound that contains at least one oxygen atom and one other element in its chemical formula. Metal oxides typically contain an anion of oxygen in the oxidation state of -2. Most of the Earth's crust consists of solid oxides, the result of elements being oxidized by the oxygen in air or in water. Hydrocarbon combustion affords the two principal carbon oxides: carbon monoxide and carbon dioxide.

Partial pressure

In a mixture of gases, each gas has a partial pressure which is the hypothetical pressure of that gas if it alone occupied the volume of the mixture at the same temperature.

The total pressure of an ideal gas mixture is the sum of the partial pressures of each individual gas in the mixture.

It relies on the following isotherm relation: $V_x \times p_{tot} = V_{tot} \times p_x$ •V_x is the partial volume of any individual gas component (X)•V_{tot} is the total volume in gas mixture•p_x is the partial pressure of gas X•p_{tot} is the total pressure of gas mixture•n_x is the amount of substance of a gas (X)•n_{tot} is the total amount of substance in gas mixture

The partial pressure of a gas is a measure of thermodynamic activity of the gas's molecules.

Total pressure

In physics, the term total pressure may indicate two different quantities, both having the dimensions of a pressure: $p_0 = p + q + \rho g z$ where ? is the density of the fluid, g is the local acceleration due to gravity, and z is the height above a datum.If the variation in height above the datum is zero, or so small it can be ignored, the above equation reduces to the following simplified form: $p_0 = p + q$ •In a mixture of ideal gases, total pressure refers to the sum of each gas' partial pressure..

Hypoxia

Hypoxia refers to low oxygen conditions. Normally 20.9% of the gas in the atmosphere is oxygen. The partial pressure of oxygen in the atmosphere is 20.9% of the total barometric pressure.

Lewis structure

Lewis structures are diagrams that show the bonding between atoms of a molecule and the lone pairs of electrons that may exist in the molecule. A Lewis structure can be drawn for any covalently bonded molecule, as well as coordination compounds. The Lewis structure was named after Gilbert N

Oxygen toxicity

Oxygen toxicity is a condition resulting from the harmful effects of breathing molecular oxygen at elevated partial pressures. It is also known as oxygen toxicity syndrome, oxygen intoxication, and oxygen poisoning. Historically, the central nervous system condition was called the Paul Bert effect, and the pulmonary condition the Lorrain Smith effect, after the researchers who pioneered its discovery and description in the late 19th century.

Vapor pressure

Vapor pressure or equilibrium vapor pressure is the pressure exerted by a vapor in thermodynamic equilibrium with its condensed phases at a given temperature in a closed system. The equilibrium vapor pressure is an indication of a liquid's evaporation rate. It relates to the tendency of particles to escape from the liquid (or a solid).

Chemical reaction

A chemical reaction is a process that leads to the transformation of one set of chemical substances to another. Classically, chemical reactions encompass changes that only involve the positions of electrons in the forming and breaking of chemical bonds between atoms, with no change to the nuclei (no change to the elements present), and can often be described by a chemical equation.

11. Gases

CHAPTER HIGHLIGHTS & NOTES: KEY TERMS, PEOPLE, PLACES, CONCEPTS

Molar volume	The molar volume, symbol V_m, is the volume occupied by one mole of a substance at a given temperature and pressure. It is equal to the molar mass (M) divided by the mass density (?). It has the SI unit cubic metres per mole (m^3/mol), although it is more practical to use the units cubic decimetres per mole (dm^3/mol) for gases and cubic centimetres per mole (cm^3/mol) for liquids and solids.
Air pollution	Air pollution is the introduction into the atmosphere of chemicals, particulates, or biological materials that cause discomfort, disease, or death to humans, damage other living organisms such as food crops, or damage the natural environment or built environment. The atmosphere is a complex dynamic natural gaseous system that is essential to support life on planet Earth. Stratospheric ozone depletion due to air pollution has long been recognized as a threat to human health as well as to the Earth's ecosystems.
Carbon monoxide	Carbon monoxide is a colorless, odorless, and tasteless gas that is slightly less dense than air. It is toxic to humans and animals when encountered in higher concentrations, although it is also produced in normal animal metabolism in low quantities, and is thought to have some normal biological functions. In the atmosphere, it is spatially variable, short lived, having a role in the formation of ground-level ozone.
Nitrogen dioxide	Nitrogen dioxide is the chemical compound with the formula NO2. It is one of several nitrogen oxides. NO2 is an intermediate in the industrial synthesis of nitric acid, millions of tons of which are produced each year.
Ozone	Ozone, or trioxygen, is an inorganic compound with the chemical formula O3(μ-O) (also written [O(μ-O)O] or O3). It is a pale blue gas with a distinctively pungent smell. It is an allotrope of oxygen that is much less stable than the diatomic allotrope O2, breaking down in the lower atmosphere to normal dioxygen.
Sulfur dioxide	Sulfur dioxide is the chemical compound with the formula SO2. At standard atmosphere it is a toxic gas with a pungent, irritating and rotten smell. The triple point is 197.69 K and 1.67Kpa.

1. In thermodynamics and fluid mechanics, _________ is a measure of the relative volume change of a fluid or solid as a response to a pressure change.

$$\beta = -\frac{1}{V}\frac{\partial V}{\partial p}$$

where V is volume and p is pressure.

a. Baroclinity
b. Barotropic fluid
c. Basset force
d. Compressibility

2. _________ is a condition resulting from the harmful effects of breathing molecular oxygen at elevated partial pressures. It is also known as _________ syndrome, oxygen intoxication, and oxygen poisoning. Historically, the central nervous system condition was called the Paul Bert effect, and the pulmonary condition the Lorrain Smith effect, after the researchers who pioneered its discovery and description in the late 19th century.

a. Bottled oxygen
b. Chemical oxygen generator
c. Compounds of oxygen
d. Oxygen toxicity

3. _________ is the property of substances to mix in all proportions, forming a homogeneous solution. The term is most often used to refer to liquids, but applies also to solids and gases. Water and ethanol, for example, are miscible because they mix in all proportions.

a. Miscibility
b. Cerium acetylacetonate
c. Dysprosium acetylacetonate
d. Gadolinium acetylacetonate

4. The early _________s were developed at the end of the 18th century, when scientists began to realize that relationships between the pressure, volume and temperature of a sample of gas could be obtained which would hold for all gases. Gases behave in a similar way over a wide variety of conditions because to a good approximation they all have molecules which are widely spaced, and nowadays the equation of state for an ideal gas is derived from kinetic theory. The earlier _________s are now considered as special cases of the ideal gas equation, with one or more of the variables held constant.

a. Merck Index
b. Buffer solution
c. Gas law
d. Carbonate alkalinity

5. . An _________ is a theoretical gas composed of a set of randomly moving, non-interacting point particles.

11. Gases

The _________ concept is useful because it obeys the _________ law, a simplified equation of state, and is amenable to analysis under statistical mechanics.

At normal conditions such as standard temperature and pressure, most real gases behave qualitatively like an _________.

a. Bisulfide
b. Buffer solution
c. Ideal gas
d. Carbonate alkalinity

ANSWER KEY
11. Gases

1. d
2. d
3. a
4. c
5. c

---

12. Liquids, Solids, and Intermolecular Forces

CHAPTER OUTLINE: KEY TERMS, PEOPLE, PLACES, CONCEPTS

- Caffeine
- Intermolecular force
- Thermal energy
- States of matter
- Glycolipid
- Phospholipid
- Steroid
- Amorphous solid
- Lewis structure
- Sodium oxide
- Density
- Surface tension
- Viscosity
- Condensation
- Evaporation
- Kinetic energy
- Dynamic equilibrium
- Vapor pressure
- Boiling point
- Endothermic
- Excited state

12. Liquids, Solids, and Intermolecular Forces

CHAPTER OUTLINE: KEY TERMS, PEOPLE, PLACES, CONCEPTS

- Vaporization
- Calcium
- Calcium oxide
- Melting point
- Heat of fusion
- Sublimation
- Carbon dioxide
- Dry ice
- Dispersion
- Ethane
- Formaldehyde
- Miscibility
- Polarization
- Petroleum
- Concentration
- Fluorine
- Methanol
- Hydrogen
- Sodium chloride
- Chloride
- Nucleotide

12. Liquids, Solids, and Intermolecular Forces

CHAPTER OUTLINE: KEY TERMS, PEOPLE, PLACES, CONCEPTS

	Ibuprofen
	Molecular solid
	Atom
	Calcium fluoride
	Xenon
	Carbon
	Mendelevium
	Carbon tetrachloride
	Drinking water
	Water pollution

CHAPTER HIGHLIGHTS & NOTES: KEY TERMS, PEOPLE, PLACES, CONCEPTS

Caffeine	Caffeine is a bitter, white crystalline xanthine alkaloid and a stimulant drug. Caffeine is found in varying quantities in the seeds, leaves, and fruit of some plants, where it acts as a natural pesticide that paralyzes and kills certain insects feeding on the plants, as well as enhancing the reward memory of pollinators. It is most commonly consumed by humans in infusions extracted from the seed of the coffee plant and the leaves of the tea bush, as well as from various foods and drinks containing products derived from the kola nut.
Intermolecular force	Intermolecular forces are forces of attraction or repulsion which act between neighboring particles . They are weak compared to the intramolecular forces, the forces which keep a molecule together. For example, the covalent bond present within HCl molecules is much stronger than the forces present between the neighboring molecules, which exist when the molecules are sufficiently close to each other.
Thermal energy	Thermal energy is the part of the total potential energy and kinetic energy of an object or sample of matter that results in the system temperature.

It is represented by the variable Q, and can be measured in Joules. This quantity may be difficult to determine or even meaningless unless the system has attained its temperature only through warming (heating), and not been subjected to work input or output, or any other energy-changing processes.

States of matter

In physics, a state of matter is one of the distinct forms that different phases of matter take on. Four states of matter are observable in everyday life: solid, liquid, gas, and plasma. Many other states are known such as Bose-Einstein condensates and neutron-degenerate matter but these only occur in extreme situations such as ultra cold or ultra dense matter.

Glycolipid

Glycolipids are lipids with a carbohydrate attached. Their role is to provide energy and also serve as markers for cellular recognition.

Phospholipid

Phospholipids are a class of lipids that are a major component of all cell membranes as they can form lipid bilayers. Most phospholipids contain a diglyceride, a phosphate group, and a simple organic molecule such as choline; one exception to this rule is sphingomyelin, which is derived from sphingosine instead of glycerol. The first phospholipid identified as such in biological tissues was lecithin, or phosphatidylcholine, in the egg yolk, by Theodore Nicolas Gobley, a French chemist and pharmacist, in 1847. The structure of the phospholipid molecule generally consists of hydrophobic tails and a hydrophilic head.

Steroid

A steroid is a type of organic compound that contains a characteristic arrangement of four cycloalkane rings that are joined to each other. Examples of steroids include the dietary fat cholesterol, the sex hormones estradiol and testosterone and the anti-inflammatory drug dexamethasone.

The core of steroids is composed of twenty carbon atoms bonded together that take the form of four fused rings: three cyclohexane rings (designated as rings A, B and C in the figure to the right) and one cyclopentane ring (the D ring).

Amorphous solid

In condensed matter physics, an amorphous or non-crystalline solid is a solid that lacks the long-range order characteristic of a crystal.

In some older books, the term has been used synonymously with glass. Nowadays, 'amorphous solid' is considered to be the overarching concept, and glass the more special case: A glass is an amorphous solid that exhibits a glass transition.

Lewis structure

Lewis structures are diagrams that show the bonding between atoms of a molecule and the lone pairs of electrons that may exist in the molecule. A Lewis structure can be drawn for any covalently bonded molecule, as well as coordination compounds. The Lewis structure was named after Gilbert N

Sodium oxide	Sodium oxide is a chemical compound with the formula Na_2O. It is used in ceramics and glasses, though not in a raw form. Treatment with water affords sodium hydroxide. $Na_2O + H_2O$? 2 NaOH The alkali metal oxides M_2O (M = Li, Na, K, Rb) crystallise in the antifluorite structure.
Density	The density, or more precisely, the volumetric mass density, of a substance is its mass per unit volume. The symbol most often used for density is ? (the lower case Greek letter rho). Mathematically, density is defined as mass divided by volume: $\rho = \frac{m}{V},$ where ? is the density, m is the mass, and V is the volume.
Surface tension	Surface tension is a contractive tendency of the surface of a liquid that allows it to resist an external force. It is revealed, for example, in the floating of some objects on the surface of water, even though they are denser than water, and in the ability of some insects (e.g. water striders) to run on the water surface. This property is caused by cohesion of similar molecules, and is responsible for many of the behaviors of liquids.
Viscosity	The viscosity of a fluid is a measure of its resistance to gradual deformation by shear stress or tensile stress. For liquids, it corresponds to the informal notion of 'thickness'. For example, honey has a higher viscosity than water.
Condensation	Condensation is the change of the physical state of matter from gas phase into liquid phase, and is the reverse of vaporization. It can also be defined as the change in the state of water vapor to water/any liquid when in contact with any surface. When the transition happens from the gaseous phase into the solid phase directly, the change is called deposition.
Evaporation	Evaporation is a type of vaporization of a liquid that occurs from the surface of a liquid into a gaseous phase that is not saturated with the evaporating substance. The other type of vaporization is boiling, which, instead, occurs within the entire mass of the liquid and can also take place when the vapor phase is saturated, such as when steam is produced in a boiler. Evaporation that occurs directly from the solid phase below the melting point, as commonly observed with ice at or below freezing or moth crystals (napthalene or paradichlorobenzine), is called sublimation.
Kinetic energy	In physics, the kinetic energy of an object is the energy which it possesses due to its motion. It is defined as the work needed to accelerate a body of a given mass from rest to its stated velocity. Having gained this energy during its acceleration, the body maintains this kinetic energy unless its speed changes.
Dynamic equilibrium	A dynamic equilibrium exists once a reversible reaction ceases to change its ratio of reactants/products, but substances move between the chemicals at an equal rate, meaning there is no net change. It is a particular example of a system in a steady state.

12. Liquids, Solids, and Intermolecular Forces

CHAPTER HIGHLIGHTS & NOTES: KEY TERMS, PEOPLE, PLACES, CONCEPTS

Vapor pressure

Vapor pressure or equilibrium vapor pressure is the pressure exerted by a vapor in thermodynamic equilibrium with its condensed phases at a given temperature in a closed system. The equilibrium vapor pressure is an indication of a liquid's evaporation rate. It relates to the tendency of particles to escape from the liquid (or a solid).

Boiling point

The boiling point of a substance is the temperature at which the vapor pressure of the liquid equals the pressure surrounding the liquid and the liquid changes into a vapor.

A liquid in a vacuum has a lower boiling point than when that liquid is at atmospheric pressure. A liquid at high-pressure has a higher boiling point than when that liquid is at atmospheric pressure.

Endothermic

In thermodynamics, the term endothermic describes a process or reaction in which the system absorbs energy from its surroundings in the form of heat. It is a modern coinage from Greek roots. The prefix endo- derives from the Greek word 'endon' (??d??) meaning 'within,' and the latter part of the word comes from the Greek word root 'therm' (?e?μ-) meaning 'hot.' The intended sense is that of a reaction that depends on taking in heat if it is to proceed.

Excited state

Excitation is an elevation in energy level above an arbitrary baseline energy state. In physics there is a specific technical definition for energy level which is often associated with an atom being excited to an excited state.

In quantum mechanics an excited state of a system (such as an atom, molecule or nucleus) is any quantum state of the system that has a higher energy than the ground state (that is, more energy than the absolute minimum).

Vaporization

Vaporization of an element or compound is a phase transition from the liquid phase to gas phase. There are two types of vaporization: evaporation and boiling.

Evaporation is a phase transition from the liquid phase to gas phase that occurs at temperatures below the boiling temperature at a given pressure.

Calcium

Calcium is the chemical element with symbol Ca and atomic number 20. Calcium is a soft gray alkaline earth metal, and is the fifth-most-abundant element by mass in the Earth's crust. Calcium is also the fifth-most-abundant dissolved ion in seawater by both molarity and mass, after sodium, chloride, magnesium, and sulfate.

Calcium is essential for living organisms, in particular in cell physiology, where movement of the calcium ion Ca^{2+} into and out of the cytoplasm functions as a signal for many cellular processes.

Calcium oxide

Calcium oxide, commonly known as quicklime or burnt lime, is a widely used chemical compound. It is a white, caustic, alkaline crystalline solid at room temperature.

Melting point

The melting point of a solid is the temperature at which it changes state from solid to liquid at atmospheric pressure. At the melting point the solid and liquid phase exist in equilibrium. The melting point of a substance depends (usually slightly) on pressure and is usually specified at standard pressure.

Heat of fusion

The enthalpy of fusion or heat of fusion is the change in enthalpy resulting from heating a given quantity of a substance to change its state from a solid to a liquid. The temperature at which this occurs is the melting point.

The 'enthalpy' of fusion is a latent heat, because during melting the introduction of heat cannot be observed as a temperature change, as the temperature remains constant during the process.

Sublimation

Sublimation is the transition of a substance directly from the solid to the gas phase without passing through an intermediate liquid phase. Sublimation is an endothermic phase transition that occurs at temperatures and pressures below a substance's triple point in its phase diagram. The reverse process of sublimation is desublimation, or deposition.

Carbon dioxide

Carbon dioxide is a naturally occurring chemical compound composed of two oxygen atoms each covalently double bonded to a single carbon atom. It is a gas at standard temperature and pressure and exists in Earth's atmosphere in this state, as a trace gas at a concentration of 0.039 per cent by volume.

As part of the carbon cycle, plants, algae, and cyanobacteria use light energy to photosynthesize carbohydrate from carbon dioxide and water, with oxygen produced as a waste product.

Dry ice

Dry ice, sometimes referred to as 'cardice' or as 'card ice', is the solid form of carbon dioxide. It is used primarily as a cooling agent. Its advantages include lower temperature than that of water ice and not leaving any residue (other than incidental frost from moisture in the atmosphere).

Dispersion

In materials science, dispersion is the fraction of atoms of a material exposed to the surface. In general: $D = N_S/N_T$

where D is the dispersion, N_S is the number of surface atoms and N_T is the total number of atoms of the material. Dispersion is an important concept in heterogeneous catalysis, since only atoms that are exposed to the surface are able to play a role in catalytic surface reactions.

Ethane

Ethane is a chemical compound with chemical formula C_2H_6. At standard temperature and pressure, ethane is a colorless, odorless gas. Ethane is isolated on an industrial scale from natural gas, and as a byproduct of petroleum refining.

Formaldehyde

Formaldehyde is an organic compound with the formula CH_2O or HCHO. It is the simplest aldehyde, hence its systematic name methanal.

The common name of the substance comes from its similarity and relation to formic acid.

A gas at room temperature, formaldehyde is colorless and has a characteristic pungent, irritating odor.

Miscibility

Miscibility is the property of substances to mix in all proportions, forming a homogeneous solution. The term is most often used to refer to liquids, but applies also to solids and gases. Water and ethanol, for example, are miscible because they mix in all proportions.

Polarization

Polarization is a property of waves that can oscillate with more than one orientation. Electromagnetic waves, such as light, and gravitational waves exhibit polarization; sound waves in a gas or liquid do not have polarization because the medium vibrates only along the direction in which the waves are travelling.

By convention, the polarization of light is described by specifying the orientation of the wave's electric field at a point in space over one period of the oscillation.

Petroleum

Petroleum (L. petroleum, from Greek: p?t?a + Latin: oleum (oil)) is a naturally occurring, smelly, yellow-to-black liquid consisting of a complex mixture of hydrocarbons of various molecular weights and other liquid organic compounds, that are found in geologic formations beneath the Earth's surface. The name Petroleum covers both naturally occurring unprocessed crude oils and petroleum products that are made up of refined crude oil. A fossil fuel, it is formed when large quantities of dead organisms, usually zooplankton and algae, are buried underneath sedimentary rock and undergo intense heat and pressure.

Concentration

In chemistry, concentration is the abundance of a constituent divided by the total volume of a mixture. Several types of mathematical description can be distinguished: mass concentration, molar concentration, number concentration, and volume concentration. The term concentration can be applied to any kind of chemical mixture, but most frequently it refers to solutes and solvents in solutions.

Fluorine

Fluorine is the chemical element with symbol F and atomic number 9. At room temperature, the element is a pale yellow gas composed of diatomic molecules, F2. Fluorine is the lightest halogen and the most electronegative element. It requires great care in handling as it is extremely reactive and poisonous.

Methanol

Methanol, also known as methyl alcohol, wood alcohol, wood naphtha or wood spirits, is a chemical with the formula CH_3OH . Methanol acquired the name 'wood alcohol' because it was once produced chiefly as a byproduct of the destructive distillation of wood. Modern methanol is produced in a catalytic industrial process directly from carbon monoxide, carbon dioxide, and hydrogen.

Hydrogen	Hydrogen is a chemical element with chemical symbol H and atomic number 1. With an atomic weight of 1.00794 u, hydrogen is the lightest element and its monatomic form (H) is the most abundant chemical substance, constituting roughly 75% of the Universe's baryonic mass. Non-remnant stars are mainly composed of hydrogen in its plasma state. At standard temperature and pressure, hydrogen is a colorless, odorless, tasteless, non-toxic, nonmetallic, highly combustible diatomic gas with the molecular formula H_2.
Sodium chloride	Sodium chloride, also known as salt, common salt, table salt or halite, is an ionic compound with the formula NaCl, representing equal proportions of sodium and chlorine. Sodium chloride is the salt most responsible for the salinity of the ocean and of the extracellular fluid of many multicellular organisms. As the major ingredient in edible salt, it is commonly used as a condiment and food preservative.
Chloride	The chloride ion is formed when the element chlorine gains an electron to form an anion (negatively charged ion) Cl^-. The salts of hydrochloric acid contain chloride ions and can also be called chlorides. The chloride ion, and its salts such as sodium chloride, are very soluble in water.
Nucleotide	Nucleotides are organic molecules that serve as the monomers, or subunits, of nucleic acids like DNA and RNA. The building blocks of nucleic acids, nucleotides are composed of a nitrogenous base, a five-carbon sugar (ribose or deoxyribose), and at least one phosphate group. Nucleotides serve to carry packets of energy within the cell (ATP). In the form of the nucleoside triphosphates (ATP, GTP, CTP and UTP), nucleotides play central roles in metabolism.
Ibuprofen	Ibuprofen is a nonsteroidal anti-inflammatory drug (NSAID) used for pain relief, fever reduction, and for reducing swelling. Ibuprofen has an antiplatelet effect, though relatively mild and somewhat short-lived compared with aspirin or prescription antiplatelet drugs. In general, ibuprofen also has a vasodilation effect.
Molecular solid	Molecular solid is a solid composed of molecules held together by the van der Waals forces. Because these dipole forces are weaker than covalent or ionic bonds, molecular solids are soft and have relatively low melting temperature. Pure molecular solids are electrical insulators but they can be made conductive by doping.
Atom	The atom is a basic unit of matter that consists of a dense central nucleus surrounded by a cloud of negatively charged electrons. The atomic nucleus contains a mix of positively charged protons and electrically neutral neutrons, which means 'uncuttable' or 'the smallest indivisible particle of matter'. Although the Indian and Greek concepts of the atom were based purely on philosophy, modern science has retained the name coined by Democritus.

12. Liquids, Solids, and Intermolecular Forces

CHAPTER HIGHLIGHTS & NOTES: KEY TERMS, PEOPLE, PLACES, CONCEPTS

Calcium fluoride	Calcium fluoride is the inorganic compound with the formula CaF_2. This ionic compound of calcium and fluorine occurs naturally as the mineral fluorite (also called fluorspar). It is the source of most of the world's fluorine.
Xenon	Xenon is a chemical element with the symbol Xe and atomic number 54. It is a colorless, heavy, odorless noble gas, that occurs in the Earth's atmosphere in trace amounts. Although generally unreactive, xenon can undergo a few chemical reactions such as the formation of xenon hexafluoroplatinate, the first noble gas compound to be synthesized. Naturally occurring xenon consists of eight stable isotopes.
Carbon	Carbon fiber, alternatively graphite fiber, carbon graphite or CF, is a material consisting of fibers about 5-10 μm in diameter and composed mostly of carbon atoms. The carbon atoms are bonded together in crystals that are more or less aligned parallel to the long axis of the fiber. The crystal alignment gives the fiber high strength-to-volume ratio (making it strong for its size).
Mendelevium	Mendelevium is a synthetic element with the symbol Md and the atomic number 101. A metallic radioactive transuranic element in the actinide series, mendelevium is usually synthesized by bombarding einsteinium with alpha particles. It was named after Dmitri Ivanovich Mendeleev, who created the periodic table, the standard way to classify all the chemical elements.
Carbon tetrachloride	Carbon tetrachloride, also known by many other names, is the organic compound with the formula CCl_4. It was formerly widely used in fire extinguishers, as a precursor to refrigerants, and as a cleaning agent. It is a colourless liquid with a 'sweet' smell that can be detected at low levels.
Drinking water	Drinking water or potable water is water safe enough to be consumed by humans or used with low risk of immediate or long term harm. In most developed countries, the water supplied to households, commerce and industry meets drinking water standards, even though only a very small proportion is actually consumed or used in food preparation. Typical uses (for other than potable purposes) include toilet flushing, washing and landscape irrigation.
Water pollution	Water pollution is the contamination of water bodies . Water pollution occurs when pollutants are directly or indirectly discharged into water bodies without adequate treatment to remove harmful compounds. Water pollution affects plants and organisms living in these bodies of water.

CHAPTER QUIZ: KEY TERMS, PEOPLE, PLACES, CONCEPTS

1. In physics, the _________ of an object is the energy which it possesses due to its motion. It is defined as the work needed to accelerate a body of a given mass from rest to its stated velocity. Having gained this energy during its acceleration, the body maintains this _________ unless its speed changes.

a. Fermi acceleration
b. Kinetic energy
c. Beat
d. Bass trap

2. _________, also known by many other names, is the organic compound with the formula CCl_4. It was formerly widely used in fire extinguishers, as a precursor to refrigerants, and as a cleaning agent. It is a colourless liquid with a 'sweet' smell that can be detected at low levels.

a. Barium chloride
b. Behentrimonium chloride
c. Carbon tetrachloride
d. Benzenediazonium chloride

3. _________ is the transition of a substance directly from the solid to the gas phase without passing through an intermediate liquid phase. _________ is an endothermic phase transition that occurs at temperatures and pressures below a substance's triple point in its phase diagram. The reverse process of _________ is de_________, or deposition.

a. Sublimation
b. Counterflow centrifugation elutriation
c. Decantation
d. Demister

4. _________ is a bitter, white crystalline xanthine alkaloid and a stimulant drug. _________ is found in varying quantities in the seeds, leaves, and fruit of some plants, where it acts as a natural pesticide that paralyzes and kills certain insects feeding on the plants, as well as enhancing the reward memory of pollinators. It is most commonly consumed by humans in infusions extracted from the seed of the coffee plant and the leaves of the tea bush, as well as from various foods and drinks containing products derived from the kola nut.

a. Caffeine
b. Xanthine
c. 2,6-Dihydroxypyridine
d. 2-Pyridone

5. . The _________, or more precisely, the volumetric mass _________, of a substance is its mass per unit volume. The symbol most often used for _________ is ? (the lower case Greek letter rho). Mathematically, _________ is defined as mass divided by volume: $\rho = \frac{m}{V}$,

where ? is the _________, m is the mass, and V is the volume.

a. Density
b. Boron trioxide
c. Calcium oxide
d. Lanthanum oxide

ANSWER KEY
12. Liquids, Solids, and Intermolecular Forces

1. b
2. c
3. a
4. a
5. a

---

13. Solutions

CHAPTER OUTLINE: KEY TERMS, PEOPLE, PLACES, CONCEPTS

Carbon dioxide

Dioxide

Aqueous solution

Blood plasma

Solvent

Homogeneous

Lewis structure

Sodium chloride

Chloride

Calcium carbonate

Saturation

Solubility

Dissociation

Precipitation

Potassium nitrate

Recrystallization

Rock candy

Straw

Mass number

Calcium

Calcium oxide

13. Solutions

CHAPTER OUTLINE: KEY TERMS, PEOPLE, PLACES, CONCEPTS

- Carbon
- Solute
- Polychlorinated biphenyl
- Dilution
- Hydrochloric acid
- Ionic compound
- Molar volume
- Stock solution
- Volume
- Stoichiometry
- Sulfuric acid
- Neutralization
- Boiling point
- Colligative properties
- Freezing point
- Antifreeze
- Ethylene glycol
- Wood frog
- Melting point
- Osmosis
- Semipermeable membrane

13. Solutions

CHAPTER OUTLINE: KEY TERMS, PEOPLE, PLACES, CONCEPTS

	Dehydration
	Osmotic pressure

CHAPTER HIGHLIGHTS & NOTES: KEY TERMS, PEOPLE, PLACES, CONCEPTS

Carbon dioxide	Carbon dioxide is a naturally occurring chemical compound composed of two oxygen atoms each covalently double bonded to a single carbon atom. It is a gas at standard temperature and pressure and exists in Earth's atmosphere in this state, as a trace gas at a concentration of 0.039 per cent by volume. As part of the carbon cycle, plants, algae, and cyanobacteria use light energy to photosynthesize carbohydrate from carbon dioxide and water, with oxygen produced as a waste product.
Dioxide	An oxide is a chemical compound that contains at least one oxygen atom and one other element in its chemical formula. Metal oxides typically contain an anion of oxygen in the oxidation state of -2. Most of the Earth's crust consists of solid oxides, the result of elements being oxidized by the oxygen in air or in water. Hydrocarbon combustion affords the two principal carbon oxides: carbon monoxide and carbon dioxide.
Aqueous solution	An aqueous solution is a solution in which the solvent is water. It is usually shown in chemical equations by appending (aq) to the relevant formula. For example, a solution of ordinary table salt, or sodium chloride (NaCl), in water would be represented as NaCl(aq).
Blood plasma	Blood plasma is the straw-colored/pale-yellow liquid component of blood that normally holds the blood cells in whole blood in suspension. It makes up about 55% of total blood volume. It is the intravascular fluid part of extracellular fluid (all body fluid outside of cells).
Solvent	A solvent is a substance that dissolves a solute (a chemically different liquid, solid or gas), resulting in a solution. A solvent is usually a liquid but can also be a solid or a gas. The maximum quantity of solute that can dissolve in a specific volume of solvent varies with temperature.
Homogeneous	Homogeneous as a term in physical chemistry and material science refers to substances and mixtures which are in a single phase. This is in contrast to a substance that is heterogeneous. The definition of homogeneous strongly depends on the context used.

13. Solutions

CHAPTER HIGHLIGHTS & NOTES: KEY TERMS, PEOPLE, PLACES, CONCEPTS

Lewis structure

Lewis structures are diagrams that show the bonding between atoms of a molecule and the lone pairs of electrons that may exist in the molecule. A Lewis structure can be drawn for any covalently bonded molecule, as well as coordination compounds. The Lewis structure was named after Gilbert N

Sodium chloride

Sodium chloride, also known as salt, common salt, table salt or halite, is an ionic compound with the formula NaCl, representing equal proportions of sodium and chlorine. Sodium chloride is the salt most responsible for the salinity of the ocean and of the extracellular fluid of many multicellular organisms. As the major ingredient in edible salt, it is commonly used as a condiment and food preservative.

Chloride

The chloride ion is formed when the element chlorine gains an electron to form an anion (negatively charged ion) Cl^-. The salts of hydrochloric acid contain chloride ions and can also be called chlorides. The chloride ion, and its salts such as sodium chloride, are very soluble in water.

Calcium carbonate

Calcium carbonate is a chemical compound with the formula $CaCO_3$. It is a common substance found in rocks in all parts of the world, and is the main component of shells of marine organisms, snails, coal balls, pearls, and eggshells. Calcium carbonate is the active ingredient in agricultural lime, and is created when Ca ions in hard water react with carbonate ions creating limescale.

Saturation

In chemistry, saturation has diverse meanings, all based on reaching a maximum capacity. •In physical chemistry, saturation is the point at which a solution of a substance can dissolve no more of that substance and additional amounts of it will appear as a separate phase (as a precipitate if solid or as effervescence or inclusion if gaseous). This point of maximum concentration, the saturation point, depends on the temperature and pressure of the solution as well as the chemical nature of the substances involved.

Solubility

Solubility is the property of a solid, liquid, or gaseous chemical substance called solute to dissolve in a solid, liquid, or gaseous solvent to form a homogeneous solution of the solute in the solvent. The solubility of a substance fundamentally depends on the physical and chemical properties of the solute and solvent as well as on temperature, pressure and the pH of the solution. The extent of the solubility of a substance in a specific solvent is measured as the saturation concentration, where adding more solute does not increase the concentration of the solution and begin to precipitate the excess amount of solute.

Dissociation

Dissociation in chemistry and biochemistry is a general process in which ionic compounds separate or split into smaller particles, ions, or radicals, usually in a reversible manner. For instance, when a Brønsted-Lowry acid is put in water, a covalent bond between an electronegative atom and a hydrogen atom is broken by heterolytic fission, which gives a proton and a negative ion. Dissociation is the opposite of association and recombination.

Precipitation

Precipitation is the formation of a solid in a solution or inside another solid during a chemical reaction or by diffusion in a solid. When the reaction occurs in a liquid solution, the solid formed is called the precipitate. The chemical that causes the solid to form is called the precipitant.

Potassium nitrate

Potassium nitrate is a chemical compound with the formula KNO_3. It is an ionic salt of potassium ions K^+ and nitrate ions NO_3^-.

It occurs as a mineral niter and is a natural solid source of nitrogen.

Recrystallization

Recrystallization is a process by which deformed grains are replaced by a new set of undeformed grains that nucleate and grow until the original grains have been entirely consumed. Recrystallization is usually accompanied by a reduction in the strength and hardness of a material and a simultaneous increase in the ductility. Thus, the process may be introduced as a deliberate step in metals processing or may be an undesirable byproduct of another processing step.

Rock candy

Rock candy is a type of confectionery mineral composed of relatively large sugar crystals. This candy is formed by allowing a supersaturated solution of sugar and water to crystallize onto a surface suitable for crystal nucleation, such as a string, stick, or plain granulated sugar. Heating the water before adding the sugar allows more sugar to dissolve thus producing larger crystals.

Straw

Straw is an agricultural by-product, the dry stalks of cereal plants, after the grain and chaff have been removed. Straw makes up about half of the yield of cereal crops such as barley, oats, rice, rye and wheat. It has many uses, including fuel, livestock bedding and fodder, thatching and basket-making.

Mass number

The mass number, also called atomic mass number or nucleon number, is the total number of protons and neutrons (together known as nucleons) in an atomic nucleus. Because protons and neutrons both are baryons, the mass number A is identical with the baryon number B as of the nucleus as of the whole atom or ion. The mass number is different for each different isotope of a chemical element.

Calcium

Calcium is the chemical element with symbol Ca and atomic number 20. Calcium is a soft gray alkaline earth metal, and is the fifth-most-abundant element by mass in the Earth's crust. Calcium is also the fifth-most-abundant dissolved ion in seawater by both molarity and mass, after sodium, chloride, magnesium, and sulfate.

Calcium is essential for living organisms, in particular in cell physiology, where movement of the calcium ion Ca^{2+} into and out of the cytoplasm functions as a signal for many cellular processes.

Calcium oxide

Calcium oxide, commonly known as quicklime or burnt lime, is a widely used chemical compound. It is a white, caustic, alkaline crystalline solid at room temperature.

13. Solutions

CHAPTER HIGHLIGHTS & NOTES: KEY TERMS, PEOPLE, PLACES, CONCEPTS

Carbon	Carbon fiber, alternatively graphite fiber, carbon graphite or CF, is a material consisting of fibers about 5-10 μm in diameter and composed mostly of carbon atoms. The carbon atoms are bonded together in crystals that are more or less aligned parallel to the long axis of the fiber. The crystal alignment gives the fiber high strength-to-volume ratio (making it strong for its size).
Solute	A solute is a substance that creates a solution when dissolved in a solvent. For example, when sugar (solute) is dissolved in water (solvent).Solute can change its physical state but solvent and solution are of same phase.e.g sugar is solid before getting dissolved in water, and after dissolution it changes its phase to a liquid. Etymology: from Latin solutus, past participle of solvere, meaning to loosen.
Polychlorinated biphenyl	Polychlorinated biphenyls were widely used as dielectric and coolant fluids, for example in transformers, capacitors, and electric motors. Due to PCBs' environmental toxicity and classification as a persistent organic pollutant, PCB production was banned by the United States Congress in 1979 and by the Stockholm Convention on Persistent Organic Pollutants in 2001. According to the U.S. Environmental Protection Agency (EPA), PCBs have been shown to cause cancer in animals, and there is also evidence that they can cause cancer in humans. A number of peer-reviewed health studies have shown an association between exposure to PCBs and non-Hodgkin Lymphoma, a frequently fatal form of cancer.
Dilution	Dilution is a reduction in the concentration of a chemical . It is the process of reducing the concentration of a solute in solution, usually simply by mixing with more solvent. To dilute a solution means to add more solvent without the addition of more solute.
Hydrochloric acid	Hydrochloric acid is a clear, colorless, highly pungent solution of hydrogen chloride in water. It is a highly corrosive, strong mineral acid with many industrial uses. Hydrochloric acid is found naturally in gastric acid.
Ionic compound	In chemistry, an ionic compound is a chemical compound in which ions are held together in a lattice structure by ionic bonds. Usually, the positively charged portion consists of metal cations and the negatively charged portion is an anion or polyatomic ion. Ions in ionic compounds are held together by the electrostatic forces between oppositely charged bodies.
Molar volume	The molar volume, symbol V_m, is the volume occupied by one mole of a substance at a given temperature and pressure. It is equal to the molar mass (M) divided by the mass density (?). It has the SI unit cubic metres per mole (m^3/mol), although it is more practical to use the units cubic decimetres per mole (dm^3/mol) for gases and cubic centimetres per mole (cm^3/mol) for liquids and solids.
Stock solution	A Stock Solution is a concentrated solution that will be diluted to some lower concentrated for actual use.

Stock solutions are used to save preparation time, conserve materials, reduce storage space, and improve the accuracy with which working lower concentration solutions are prepared.

In chemistry, a stock solution is a large volume of a common reagent, such as hydrochloric acid or sodium hydroxide, at a standardized concentration.

Volume

In thermodynamics, the volume of a system is an important extensive parameter for describing its thermodynamic state. The specific volume, an intensive property, is the system's volume per unit of mass. Volume is a function of state and is interdependent with other thermodynamic properties such as pressure and temperature.

Stoichiometry

Stoichiometry is a branch of chemistry that deals with the relative quantities of reactants and products in chemical reactions. In a balanced chemical reaction, the relations among quantities of reactants and products typically form a ratio of positive integers. For example, in a reaction that forms ammonia (NH_3), exactly one molecule of nitrogen gas (N_2) reacts with three molecules of hydrogen gas (H_2) to produce two molecules of NH_3:N2 + 3H2 ? 2NH3

This particular kind of stoichiometry - describing the quantitative relationships among substances as they participate in chemical reactions - is known as reaction stoichiometry.

Sulfuric acid

Sulfuric acid is a highly corrosive strong mineral acid with the molecular formula H_2SO_4. It is a pungent, colorless to slightly yellow viscous liquid which is soluble in water at all concentrations. Sometimes, it is dyed dark brown during production to alert people to its hazards

Neutralization

In chemistry, neutralization is a chemical reaction in which an acid and a base react to form a salt. Water is frequently, but not necessarily, produced as well. Neutralizations with Arrhenius acids and bases always produce water where acid-alkali reactions produce water and a metal salt.

Boiling point

The boiling point of a substance is the temperature at which the vapor pressure of the liquid equals the pressure surrounding the liquid and the liquid changes into a vapor.

A liquid in a vacuum has a lower boiling point than when that liquid is at atmospheric pressure. A liquid at high-pressure has a higher boiling point than when that liquid is at atmospheric pressure.

Colligative properties

In chemistry, colligative properties are properties of solutions that depend upon the ratio of the number of solute particles to the number of solvent molecules in a solution, and not on the type of chemical species present. This number ratio can be related to the various units for concentration of solutions. Here we shall only consider those properties which result because of the dissolution of nonvolatile solute in a volatile liquid solvent.

Freezing point

Freezing, or Solidification, is a phase transition in which a liquid turns into a solid when its temperature is lowered below its freezing point.

For most substances, the melting and freezing points are the same temperature; however, certain substances possess differing solid-liquid transition temperatures. For example, agar displays a hysteresis in its melting and freezing temperatures.

Antifreeze

An antifreeze is a chemical additive which lowers the freezing point of a water-based liquid. An antifreeze mixture is used to achieve freezing-point depression for cold environments and also achieves boiling-point elevation ('anti-boil') to allow higher coolant temperature. Freezing and boiling points are colligative properties of a solution, which depend on the concentration of the dissolved substance.

Ethylene glycol

Ethylene glycol is an organic compound primarily used as a raw material in the manufacture of polyester fibers and fabric industry, and polyethylene terephthalate resins (PET) used in bottling. A small percent is also used in industrial applications like antifreeze formulations and other industrial products. It is an odorless, colorless, syrupy, sweet-tasting liquid.

Wood frog

The Asian Kokarit Frog is occasionally also called 'wood frog', particularly when listed under its junior synonym Rana nigrolineata.

The wood frog has a broad distribution over North America, extending from the southern Appalachians to the boreal forest with several notable disjunct populations including lowland eastern North Carolina. The wood frog has garnered attention by biologists over the last century because of its freeze tolerance, relatively great degree of terrestrialism (for a Ranid), interesting habitat associations (peat bogs, vernal pools, uplands), and relatively long-range movements. The ecology and conservation of the wood frog has attracted a great deal of research attention in recent years.

Melting point

The melting point of a solid is the temperature at which it changes state from solid to liquid at atmospheric pressure. At the melting point the solid and liquid phase exist in equilibrium. The melting point of a substance depends (usually slightly) on pressure and is usually specified at standard pressure.

Osmosis

Osmosis is the spontaneous net movement of solvent molecules through a partially permeable membrane into a region of higher solute concentration, in the direction that tends to equalize the solute concentrations on the two sides. It may also be used to describe a physical process in which any solvent moves, without input of energy, across a semipermeable membrane (permeable to the solvent, but not the solute) separating two solutions of different concentrations. Although osmosis does not require input of energy, it does use kinetic energy and can be made to do work.

13. Solutions

CHAPTER HIGHLIGHTS & NOTES: KEY TERMS, PEOPLE, PLACES, CONCEPTS

Semipermeable membrane	A semipermeable membrane, also termed a selectively permeable membrane, a partially permeable membrane or a differentially permeable membrane, is a membrane that will allow certain molecules or ions to pass through it by diffusion and occasionally specialized 'facilitated diffusion'. Prof. Sidney Loeb and Srinivasa Sourirajan invented the first practical synthetic semi-permeable membrane.
Dehydration	In physiology and medicine, dehydration is the excessive loss of body water, with an accompanying disruption of metabolic processes. It is literally the removal of water (Ancient Greek: ?d?? hýdor) from an object; however, in physiological terms, it entails a deficiency of fluid within an organism. Dehydration of skin and mucous membranes can be called medical dryness.
Osmotic pressure	Osmotic pressure is the pressure which needs to be applied to a solution to prevent the inward flow of water across a semipermeable membrane. It is also defined as the minimum pressure needed to nullify osmosis. The phenomenon of osmotic pressure arises from the tendency of a pure solvent to move through a semi-permeable membrane and into a solution containing a solute to which the membrane is impermeable.

CHAPTER QUIZ: KEY TERMS, PEOPLE, PLACES, CONCEPTS

1. _________ is a naturally occurring chemical compound composed of two oxygen atoms each covalently double bonded to a single carbon atom. It is a gas at standard temperature and pressure and exists in Earth's atmosphere in this state, as a trace gas at a concentration of 0.039 per cent by volume.

   As part of the carbon cycle, plants, algae, and cyanobacteria use light energy to photosynthesize carbohydrate from _________ and water, with oxygen produced as a waste product.

   a. Barium acetylacetonate
   b. Cerium acetylacetonate
   c. Carbon dioxide
   d. Gadolinium acetylacetonate

2. . _________ is the property of a solid, liquid, or gaseous chemical substance called solute to dissolve in a solid, liquid, or gaseous solvent to form a homogeneous solution of the solute in the solvent. The _________ of a substance fundamentally depends on the physical and chemical properties of the solute and solvent as well as on temperature, pressure and the pH of the solution. The extent of the _________ of a substance in a specific solvent is measured as the saturation concentration, where adding more solute does not increase the concentration of the solution and begin to precipitate the excess amount of solute.

a. Solubility
b. Concentrate
c. Condosity
d. Crenation

3. The Asian Kokarit Frog is occasionally also called '_________', particularly when listed under its junior synonym Rana nigrolineata.

The _________ has a broad distribution over North America, extending from the southern Appalachians to the boreal forest with several notable disjunct populations including lowland eastern North Carolina. The _________ has garnered attention by biologists over the last century because of its freeze tolerance, relatively great degree of terrestrialism (for a Ranid), interesting habitat associations (peat bogs, vernal pools, uplands), and relatively long-range movements. The ecology and conservation of the _________ has attracted a great deal of research attention in recent years.

a. Cryozoa
b. Wood frog
c. Painted turtle
d. Siberian salamander

4. A _________ is a substance that dissolves a solute (a chemically different liquid, solid or gas), resulting in a solution. A _________ is usually a liquid but can also be a solid or a gas. The maximum quantity of solute that can dissolve in a specific volume of _________ varies with temperature.

a. Bioorthogonal chemistry
b. Solvent
c. Carbothermic reaction
d. Ceramide phosphoethanolamine synthase

5. _________ is a type of confectionery mineral composed of relatively large sugar crystals. This candy is formed by allowing a supersaturated solution of sugar and water to crystallize onto a surface suitable for crystal nucleation, such as a string, stick, or plain granulated sugar. Heating the water before adding the sugar allows more sugar to dissolve thus producing larger crystals.

a. Rock candy
b. Bismuth germanate
c. Boule
d. Caesium cadmium bromide

ANSWER KEY
13. Solutions

---

1. c

2. a

3. b

4. b

5. a

---

14. Acids and Bases

CHAPTER OUTLINE: KEY TERMS, PEOPLE, PLACES, CONCEPTS

- Oxide
- Hydrochloric acid
- Acetic acid
- Carboxylic acid
- Citric acid
- Malic acid
- Nitric acid
- Sulfuric acid
- Alkaloid
- Ammonia
- Drano
- Potassium hydroxide
- Sodium bicarbonate
- Sodium hydroxide
- Dissociation
- Formic acid
- Ionic compound
- Ionization
- Molar volume
- Concentration
- Volume

14. Acids and Bases

CHAPTER OUTLINE: KEY TERMS, PEOPLE, PLACES, CONCEPTS

- Potassium
- Bicarbonate
- Carbon dioxide
- Magnesium chloride
- Magnesium
- Neutralization
- Sodium
- Gold
- Hydrobromic acid
- Magnesium bromide
- Magnesium oxide
- Potassium chloride
- Potassium oxide
- Zinc
- Lewis structure
- Titration
- Hydroxide
- Radiation
- Equivalence point
- Phenolphthalein
- Strength

14. Acids and Bases

CHAPTER OUTLINE: KEY TERMS, PEOPLE, PLACES, CONCEPTS

- Conductivity
- Diprotic acid
- Electrolyte
- Hydrofluoric acid
- Strong electrolyte
- Carbonic acid
- Hydronium
- Phosphoric acid
- Sulfurous acid
- Weak base
- Atom
- Buffer
- Caffeine
- Morphine
- Narcotic
- Nicotine
- Sodium acetate
- Antifreeze
- Ethylene glycol
- Glycolic acid

14. Acids and Bases

CHAPTER HIGHLIGHTS & NOTES: KEY TERMS, PEOPLE, PLACES, CONCEPTS

Oxide	An oxide is a chemical compound that contains at least one oxygen atom and one other element in its chemical formula. Metal oxides typically contain an anion of oxygen in the oxidation state of -2. Most of the Earth's crust consists of solid oxides, the result of elements being oxidized by the oxygen in air or in water. Hydrocarbon combustion affords the two principal carbon oxides: carbon monoxide and carbon dioxide.
Hydrochloric acid	Hydrochloric acid is a clear, colorless, highly pungent solution of hydrogen chloride in water. It is a highly corrosive, strong mineral acid with many industrial uses. Hydrochloric acid is found naturally in gastric acid.
Acetic acid	Acetic acid is an organic compound with the chemical formula CH_3COOH (also written as CH_3CO_2H or $C_2H_4O_2$). It is a colourless liquid that when undiluted is also called glacial acetic acid. Acetic acid is the main component of vinegar (apart from water; vinegar is roughly 8% acetic acid by volume), and has a distinctive sour taste and pungent smell.
Carboxylic acid	A carboxylic acid is an organic acid characterized by the presence of at least one carboxyl group. The general formula of a carboxylic acid is R-COOH, where R is some monovalent functional group. A carboxyl group (or carboxy) is a functional group consisting of a carbonyl (RR'C=O) and a hydroxyl (R-O-H), which has the formula -C(=O)OH, usually written as -COOH or $-CO_2H$. Carboxylic acids are Brønsted-Lowry acids because they are proton (H^+) donors.
Citric acid	Citric acid is a weak organic acid with the formula $C_6H_8O_7$. It is a natural preservative/conservative and is also used to add an acidic or sour taste to foods and drinks. In biochemistry, the conjugate base of citric acid, citrate, is important as an intermediate in the citric acid cycle, which occurs in the metabolism of all aerobic organisms.
Malic acid	Malic acid is an organic compound with the formula $HO_2CCH_2CHOHCO_2H$. It is a dicarboxylic acid that is made by all living organisms, contributes to the pleasantly sour taste of fruits, and is used as a food additive. Malic acid has two stereoisomeric forms (- and -enantiomers), though only the - isomer exists naturally. The salts and esters of malic acid are known as malates.
Nitric acid	Nitric acid, also known as aqua fortis and spirit of niter, is a highly corrosive strong mineral acid. The pure compound is colorless, but older samples tend to acquire a yellow cast due to decomposition into oxides of nitrogen and water. Most commercially available nitric acid has a concentration of 68%.
Sulfuric acid	Sulfuric acid is a highly corrosive strong mineral acid with the molecular formula H_2SO_4. It is a pungent, colorless to slightly yellow viscous liquid which is soluble in water at all concentrations. Sometimes, it is dyed dark brown during production to alert people to its hazards.

Alkaloid	Alkaloids are a group of naturally occurring chemical compounds, that contain mostly basic nitrogen atoms. This group also includes some related compounds with neutral and even weakly acidic properties. Some synthetic compounds of similar structure are also attributed to alkaloids.
Ammonia	Ammonia or azane is a compound of nitrogen and hydrogen with the formula NH_3. It is a colourless gas with a characteristic pungent smell. Ammonia contributes significantly to the nutritional needs of terrestrial organisms by serving as a precursor to food and fertilizers.
Drano	Drano is a drain cleaner product manufactured by S. C. Johnson & Son.
Potassium hydroxide	Potassium hydroxide is an inorganic compound with the formula KOH, commonly called caustic potash. Along with sodium hydroxide, this colorless solid is a prototypical strong base. It has many industrial and niche applications; most applications exploit its reactivity toward acids and its corrosive nature.
Sodium bicarbonate	Sodium bicarbonate or sodium hydrogen carbonate is the chemical compound with the formula $NaHCO_3$. Sodium bicarbonate is a white solid that is crystalline but often appears as a fine powder. It has a slightly salty, alkaline taste resembling that of washing soda (sodium carbonate).
Sodium hydroxide	Sodium hydroxide, also known as caustic soda, or lye, is an inorganic compound with the chemical formula NaOH . It is a white solid, and is a highly caustic metallic base and alkali salt. It is available in pellets, flakes, granules, and as prepared solutions at a number of different concentrations.
Dissociation	Dissociation in chemistry and biochemistry is a general process in which ionic compounds separate or split into smaller particles, ions, or radicals, usually in a reversible manner. For instance, when a Brønsted-Lowry acid is put in water, a covalent bond between an electronegative atom and a hydrogen atom is broken by heterolytic fission, which gives a proton and a negative ion. Dissociation is the opposite of association and recombination.
Formic acid	Formic acid is the simplest carboxylic acid. Its chemical formula is HCOOH or HCO_2H. It is an important intermediate in chemical synthesis and occurs naturally, most notably in ant venom. In fact, its name comes from the Latin word for ant, formica, referring to its early isolation by the distillation of ant bodies.
Ionic compound	In chemistry, an ionic compound is a chemical compound in which ions are held together in a lattice structure by ionic bonds. Usually, the positively charged portion consists of metal cations and the negatively charged portion is an anion or polyatomic ion. Ions in ionic compounds are held together by the electrostatic forces between oppositely charged bodies.

14. Acids and Bases

Ionization	Ionization is the process by which an atom or a molecule acquires a negative or positive charge by gaining or losing electrons.
Molar volume	The molar volume, symbol V_m, is the volume occupied by one mole of a substance at a given temperature and pressure. It is equal to the molar mass (M) divided by the mass density (?). It has the SI unit cubic metres per mole (m^3/mol), although it is more practical to use the units cubic decimetres per mole (dm^3/mol) for gases and cubic centimetres per mole (cm^3/mol) for liquids and solids.
Concentration	In chemistry, concentration is the abundance of a constituent divided by the total volume of a mixture. Several types of mathematical description can be distinguished: mass concentration, molar concentration, number concentration, and volume concentration. The term concentration can be applied to any kind of chemical mixture, but most frequently it refers to solutes and solvents in solutions.
Volume	In thermodynamics, the volume of a system is an important extensive parameter for describing its thermodynamic state. The specific volume, an intensive property, is the system's volume per unit of mass. Volume is a function of state and is interdependent with other thermodynamic properties such as pressure and temperature.
Potassium	Potassium is a chemical element with symbol K and atomic number 19. Elemental potassium is a soft silvery-white alkali metal that oxidizes rapidly in air and is very reactive with water, generating sufficient heat to ignite the hydrogen emitted in the reaction and burning with a lilac flame. Because potassium and sodium are chemically very similar, their salts were not at first differentiated. The existence of multiple elements in their salts was suspected from 1702, and this was proven in 1807 when potassium and sodium were individually isolated from different salts by electrolysis.
Bicarbonate	In inorganic chemistry, bicarbonate is an intermediate form in the deprotonation of carbonic acid. It is an anion with the chemical formula HCO_3^-. Bicarbonate serves a crucial biochemical role in the physiological pH buffering system.
Carbon dioxide	Carbon dioxide is a naturally occurring chemical compound composed of two oxygen atoms each covalently double bonded to a single carbon atom. It is a gas at standard temperature and pressure and exists in Earth's atmosphere in this state, as a trace gas at a concentration of 0.039 per cent by volume.

Magnesium chloride	Magnesium chloride is the name for the chemical compounds with the formulas $MgCl_2$ and its various hydrates $MgCl_{2x}$. These salts are typical ionic halides, being highly soluble in water. The hydrated magnesium chloride can be extracted from brine or sea water.
Magnesium	Magnesium is a chemical element with the symbol Mg and atomic number 12. Its common oxidation number is +2. It is an alkaline earth metal and the eighth most abundant element in the Earth's crust and ninth in the known universe as a whole. Magnesium is the fourth most common element in the Earth as a whole (behind iron, oxygen and silicon), making up 13% of the planet's mass and a large fraction of the planet's mantle. The relative abundance of magnesium is related to the fact that it easily builds up in supernova stars from a sequential addition of three helium nuclei to carbon (which in turn is made from three helium nuclei).
Neutralization	In chemistry, neutralization is a chemical reaction in which an acid and a base react to form a salt. Water is frequently, but not necessarily, produced as well. Neutralizations with Arrhenius acids and bases always produce water where acid-alkali reactions produce water and a metal salt.
Sodium	Sodium is a chemical element with the symbol Na and atomic number 11. It is a soft, silver-white, highly reactive metal and is a member of the alkali metals; its only stable isotope is ^{23}Na. The free metal does not occur in nature, but instead must be prepared from its compounds; it was first isolated by Humphry Davy in 1807 by the electrolysis of sodium hydroxide. Sodium is the sixth most abundant element in the Earth's crust, and exists in numerous minerals such as feldspars, sodalite and rock salt.
Gold	Gold is a chemical element with the symbol Au and atomic number 79. It is a dense, soft, malleable, and ductile metal with an attractive, bright yellow color and luster that is maintained without tarnishing in air or water. Chemically, gold is a transition metal and a group 11 element. It is one of the least reactive chemical elements, solid under standard conditions.
Hydrobromic acid	Hydrobromic acid is a strong acid formed by dissolving the diatomic molecule hydrogen bromide in water. 'Constant boiling' hydrobromic acid is an aqueous solution that distills at 124.3 °C and contains 47.6% HBr by weight, which is 8.89 mol/L. Hydrobromic acid has a pK_a of -9, making it a stronger acid than hydrochloric acid, but not as strong as hydroiodic acid. Hydrobromic acid is one of the strongest mineral acids known.
Magnesium bromide	Magnesium bromide is a chemical compound of magnesium and bromine that is white and deliquescent. It is often used as a mild sedative and as an anticonvulsant for treatment of nervous disorders. It is water soluble and somewhat soluble in alcohol.
Magnesium oxide	Magnesium oxide, or magnesia, is a white hygroscopic solid mineral that occurs naturally as periclase and is a source of magnesium . It has an empirical formula of MgO and consists of a lattice of Mg^{2+} ions and O^{2-} ions held together by ionic bonding.

14. Acids and Bases

CHAPTER HIGHLIGHTS & NOTES: KEY TERMS, PEOPLE, PLACES, CONCEPTS

Potassium chloride	The chemical compound potassium chloride is a metal halide salt composed of potassium and chlorine. In its pure state, it is odorless and has a white or colorless vitreous crystal appearance, with a crystal structure that cleaves easily in three directions. Potassium chloride crystals are face-centered cubic.
Potassium oxide	Potassium oxide is an ionic compound of potassium and oxygen. This pale yellow solid, the simplest oxide of potassium, is a rarely encountered, highly reactive compound. Some materials of commerce, such as fertilizers and cements, are assayed assuming the percent composition that would be equivalent to K_2O.
Zinc	Zinc, in commerce also spelter, is a metallic chemical element; it has the symbol Zn and atomic number 30. It is the first element of group 12 of the periodic table. Zinc is, in some respects, chemically similar to magnesium, because its ion is of similar size and its only common oxidation state is +2. Zinc is the 24th most abundant element in the Earth's crust and has five stable isotopes. The most common zinc ore is sphalerite (zinc blende), a zinc sulfide mineral.
Lewis structure	Lewis structures are diagrams that show the bonding between atoms of a molecule and the lone pairs of electrons that may exist in the molecule. A Lewis structure can be drawn for any covalently bonded molecule, as well as coordination compounds. The Lewis structure was named after Gilbert N
Titration	Titration, also known as titrimetry, is a common laboratory method of quantitative chemical analysis that is used to determine the unknown concentration of an identified analyte. Since volume measurements play a key role in titration, it is also known as volumetric analysis. A reagent, called the titrant or titrator is prepared as a standard solution.
Hydroxide	Hydroxide is a diatomic anion with chemical formula OH^-. It consists of an oxygen and a hydrogen atom held together by a covalent bond, and carries a negative electric charge. It is an important but usually minor constituent of water.
Radiation	In physics, radiation is a process in which energetic particles or energetic waves travel through a vacuum, or through matter-containing media that are not required for their propagation. Waves of a mass filled medium itself, such as water waves or sound waves, are usually not considered to be forms of 'radiation' in this sense. Radiation can be classified as either ionizing or non-ionizing according to whether it ionizes or does not ionize ordinary chemical matter.
Equivalence point	The equivalence point, or stoichiometric point, of a chemical reaction is the point at which an added titrant is stoichiometrically equal to the number of moles of substance present in the sample: the smallest amount of titrant that is sufficient to fully neutralize or react with the analyte.

In some cases there are multiple equivalence points, which are multiples of the first equivalence point, such as in the titration of a diprotic acid.

Acid-Base Equivalence Point - the point at which chemically equivalent quantities of acid and base have been mixed, can be found by means of an indicator

In a reaction, the equivalence of the reactants as well as products is conserved.

Phenolphthalein

Phenolphthalein is a chemical compound with the formula $C_{20}H_{14}O_4$ and is often written as 'HIn' or 'phph' in shorthand notation. Often used in titrations, it turns colorless in acidic solutions and pink in basic solutions. If the concentration of indicator is particularly strong, it can appear purple.

Strength

In explosive materials, strength is the parameter determining the ability of the explosive to move the surrounding material. It is related to the total gas yield of the reaction, and the amount of heat produced. Cf.

Conductivity

The conductivity of an electrolyte solution is a measure of its ability to conduct electricity. The SI unit of conductivity is siemens per meter (S/m).

Conductivity measurements are used routinely in many industrial and environmental applications as a fast, inexpensive and reliable way of measuring the ionic content in a solution.

Diprotic acid

A diprotic acid is an acid such as H_2SO_4 that contains within its molecular structure two hydrogen atoms per molecule capable of dissociating (i.e. ionizable) in water. The complete dissociation of diprotic acids is of the same form as sulfuric acid:H_2SO_4 ? $H^+(aq) + HSO_4^-(aq)$ $K_a = 1 \times 10^3$$HSO_4^-$? $H^+(aq) + SO_4^{2-}(aq)$ $K_a = 1 \times 10^{-2}$

The dissociation does not happen all at once due to the two stages of dissociation having different K_a values. The first dissociation will, in the case of sulfuric acid, occur completely, but the second one will not.

Electrolyte

An electrolyte is a compound that ionizes when dissolved in suitable ionizing solvents such as water. This includes most soluble salts, acids, and bases. Some gases, such as hydrogen chloride, under conditions of high temperature or low pressure can also function as electrolytes.

Hydrofluoric acid

Hydrofluoric acid is a solution of hydrogen fluoride in water. It is a valued source of fluorine and is a precursor to numerous pharmaceuticals such as fluoxetine (Prozac) and diverse materials such as PTFE (Teflon).

Hydrofluoric acid is a highly corrosive acid, capable of dissolving many materials, especially oxides.

14. Acids and Bases

CHAPTER HIGHLIGHTS & NOTES: KEY TERMS, PEOPLE, PLACES, CONCEPTS

Strong electrolyte

A strong electrolyte is a solute that completely, or almost completely, ionizes or dissociates in a solution. These ions are good conductors of electric current in the solution.

Originally, a 'strong electrolyte' was defined as a chemical that, when in aqueous solution, is a good conductor of electricity.

Carbonic acid

Not to be confused with carbolic acid, an antiquated name for phenol.Carbonic acid is also an archaic name for carbon dioxide.

Carbonic acid is the chemical compound with the formula H_2CO_3 (equivalently OC_2). It is also a name sometimes given to solutions of carbon dioxide in water (carbonated water), because such solutions contain small amounts of H_2CO_3. Carbonic acid, which is a weak acid, forms two kinds of salts, the carbonates and the bicarbonates.

Hydronium

The hydronium cation, also known as hydroxonium is the positively charged polyatomic ion with the chemical formula H3O+. Hydronium, a type of oxonium ion, is formed by the protonation of water (H2O). This cation is often used to represent the nature of the proton in aqueous solution, where the proton is highly solvated (bound to a solvent).

Phosphoric acid

Phosphoric acid is a mineral (inorganic) acid having the chemical formula H_3PO_4. Orthophosphoric acid molecules can combine with themselves to form a variety of compounds which are also referred to as phosphoric acids, but in a more general way. The term phosphoric acid can also refer to a chemical or reagent consisting of phosphoric acids, such as pyrophosphoric acid or triphosphoric acid, but usually orthophosphoric acid.

Sulfurous acid

Sulfurous acid is the chemical compound with the formula H_2SO_3. There is no evidence that sulfurous acid exists in solution, but the molecule has been detected in the gas phase. The conjugate bases of this elusive acid are, however, common anions, bisulfite (or hydrogensulfite) and sulfite.

Weak base

In chemistry, a weak base is a chemical base that does not ionize fully in an aqueous solution. As Brønsted-Lowry bases are proton acceptors, a weak base may also be defined as a chemical base in which protonation is incomplete. This results in a relatively low pH compared to strong bases.

Atom

The atom is a basic unit of matter that consists of a dense central nucleus surrounded by a cloud of negatively charged electrons. The atomic nucleus contains a mix of positively charged protons and electrically neutral neutrons, which means 'uncuttable' or 'the smallest indivisible particle of matter'. Although the Indian and Greek concepts of the atom were based purely on philosophy, modern science has retained the name coined by Democritus.

Buffer	In a fiber optic cable, a buffer is one type of component used to encapsulate one or more optical fibers for the purpose of providing such functions as mechanical isolation, protection from physical damage and fiber identification. The buffer may take the form of a miniature conduit, contained within the cable and called a 'loose buffer', or 'loose buffer tube'. A loose buffer may contain more than one fiber, and sometimes contains a lubricating gel.
Caffeine	Caffeine is a bitter, white crystalline xanthine alkaloid and a stimulant drug. Caffeine is found in varying quantities in the seeds, leaves, and fruit of some plants, where it acts as a natural pesticide that paralyzes and kills certain insects feeding on the plants, as well as enhancing the reward memory of pollinators. It is most commonly consumed by humans in infusions extracted from the seed of the coffee plant and the leaves of the tea bush, as well as from various foods and drinks containing products derived from the kola nut.
Morphine	Morphine for its tendency to cause sleep. After it was isolated from opium by Sertürner, the traditional way to obtain morphine had been by chemical processing of opium. In India, opium harvested by licensed poppy farmers is dehydrated to uniform levels of hydration at government processing centers, and then sold to pharmaceutical companies, which extract morphine from the opium.
Narcotic	The term narcotic originally referred medically to any psychoactive compound with any sleep-inducing properties. In the US it has since become associated with opioids, commonly morphine and heroin and their derivatives, such as hydrocodone. The term is, today, imprecisely defined and typically has negative connotations.
Nicotine	Nicotine is a potent parasympathomimetic alkaloid found in the nightshade family of plants and a stimulant drug. It is a nicotinic acetylcholine receptor agonist. It is made in the roots and accumulates in the leaves of the plants.
Sodium acetate	Sodium acetate, CH_3COONa, also abbreviated NaOAc, also sodium ethanoate, is the sodium salt of acetic acid. This colourless salt has a wide range of uses.
Antifreeze	An antifreeze is a chemical additive which lowers the freezing point of a water-based liquid. An antifreeze mixture is used to achieve freezing-point depression for cold environments and also achieves boiling-point elevation ('anti-boil') to allow higher coolant temperature. Freezing and boiling points are colligative properties of a solution, which depend on the concentration of the dissolved substance.
Ethylene glycol	Ethylene glycol is an organic compound primarily used as a raw material in the manufacture of polyester fibers and fabric industry, and polyethylene terephthalate resins (PET) used in bottling.

14. Acids and Bases

CHAPTER HIGHLIGHTS & NOTES: KEY TERMS, PEOPLE, PLACES, CONCEPTS

A small percent is also used in industrial applications like antifreeze formulations and other industrial products. It is an odorless, colorless, syrupy, sweet-tasting liquid.

Glycolic acid — Glycolic acid is the smallest a-hydroxy acid (AHA). This colorless, odorless, and hygroscopic crystalline solid is highly soluble in water. It is used in various skin-care products.

CHAPTER QUIZ: KEY TERMS, PEOPLE, PLACES, CONCEPTS

1. In chemistry, _________ is the abundance of a constituent divided by the total volume of a mixture. Several types of mathematical description can be distinguished: mass _________, molar _________, number _________, and volume _________. The term _________ can be applied to any kind of chemical mixture, but most frequently it refers to solutes and solvents in solutions.

   a. Biomonitoring
   b. Concentration
   c. Bradford protein assay
   d. Bulk material analyzer

2. An _________ is a chemical compound that contains at least one oxygen atom and one other element in its chemical formula. Metal _________s typically contain an anion of oxygen in the oxidation state of -2. Most of the Earth's crust consists of solid _________s, the result of elements being oxidized by the oxygen in air or in water. Hydrocarbon combustion affords the two principal carbon _________s: carbon mon_________ and carbon di_________.

   a. Bifluoride
   b. Bismuthide
   c. Bisulfide
   d. Oxide

3. _________ or sodium hydrogen carbonate is the chemical compound with the formula $NaHCO_3$. _________ is a white solid that is crystalline but often appears as a fine powder. It has a slightly salty, alkaline taste resembling that of washing soda (sodium carbonate).

   a. Sodium bicarbonate
   b. Base modifying agent
   c. Calcium oxide
   d. Free base

4. . _________s are a group of naturally occurring chemical compounds, that contain mostly basic nitrogen atoms.

This group also includes some related compounds with neutral and even weakly acidic properties Some synthetic compounds of similar structure are also attributed to _________s.

a. 2,6-Dihydroxypyridine
b. 2-Pyridone
c. Ciclopirox
d. Alkaloid

5. _________ is a drain cleaner product manufactured by S. C. Johnson & Son.

a. 2-Butoxyethanol
b. Balalaikalate
c. Drano
d. Behold

ANSWER KEY
14. Acids and Bases

---

1. b
2. d
3. a
4. d
5. c

You can take the complete Chapter Practice Test

for 14. Acids and Bases
on all key terms, persons, places, and concepts.

Online 99 Cents

http://www.JustTheFacts101.com

Use www.JustTheFacts101.com for all your study needs including Facts101's online interactive problem solving labs in chemistry, statistics, mathematics, and more.

15. Chemical Equilibrium

CHAPTER OUTLINE: KEY TERMS, PEOPLE, PLACES, CONCEPTS

- Dynamic equilibrium
- Lewis structure
- Collision theory
- Activation
- Activation energy
- Chemical reaction
- Hydrogen
- Iodine
- Logarithm
- Concentration
- Reversible reaction
- Equilibrium constant
- Carbon
- Glycolipid
- Phospholipid
- Steroid
- Calcium
- Calcium oxide
- Ideal gas
- Ideal gas law
- Volume

15. Chemical Equilibrium

CHAPTER OUTLINE: KEY TERMS, PEOPLE, PLACES, CONCEPTS

Hemoglobin

Oxygen

Excited state

Nitrite

Nitrogen

Molar solubility

Silver chloride

Hard water

Carbon monoxide

Catalyst

Chlorofluorocarbon

Ozone

Enzyme

15. Chemical Equilibrium

CHAPTER HIGHLIGHTS & NOTES: KEY TERMS, PEOPLE, PLACES, CONCEPTS

Dynamic equilibrium	A dynamic equilibrium exists once a reversible reaction ceases to change its ratio of reactants/products, but substances move between the chemicals at an equal rate, meaning there is no net change. It is a particular example of a system in a steady state. In thermodynamics a closed system is in thermodynamic equilibrium when reactions occur at such rates that the composition of the mixture does not change with time.
Lewis structure	Lewis structures are diagrams that show the bonding between atoms of a molecule and the lone pairs of electrons that may exist in the molecule. A Lewis structure can be drawn for any covalently bonded molecule, as well as coordination compounds. The Lewis structure was named after Gilbert N
Collision theory	Collision theory is a theory proposed independently by Max Trautz in 1916 and William Lewis in 1918, that qualitatively explains how chemical reactions occur and why reaction rates differ for different reactions. The collision theory states that when suitable particles of the reactant hit each other, only a certain percentage of the collisions cause any noticeable or significant chemical change; these successful changes are called successful collisions. The successful collisions have enough energy, also known as activation energy, at the moment of impact to break the preexisting bonds and form all new bonds.
Activation	Activation in chemical sciences generally refers to the process whereby something is prepared or excited for a subsequent reaction.
Activation energy	In chemistry, activation energy is a term introduced in 1889 by the Swedish scientist Svante Arrhenius that is defined as the minimum energy that must be input to a chemical system, containing potential reactants, in order for a chemical reaction to occur. Activation energy may also be defined as the minimum energy required to start a chemical reaction. The activation energy of a reaction is usually denoted by E_a and given in units of kilojoules per mole.
Chemical reaction	A chemical reaction is a process that leads to the transformation of one set of chemical substances to another. Classically, chemical reactions encompass changes that only involve the positions of electrons in the forming and breaking of chemical bonds between atoms, with no change to the nuclei (no change to the elements present), and can often be described by a chemical equation. Nuclear chemistry is a sub-discipline of chemistry that involves the chemical reactions of unstable and radioactive elements where both electronic and nuclear changes may both occur.
Hydrogen	Hydrogen is a chemical element with chemical symbol H and atomic number 1. With an atomic weight of 1.00794 u, hydrogen is the lightest element and its monatomic form (H) is the most abundant chemical substance, constituting roughly 75% of the Universe's baryonic mass. Non-remnant stars are mainly composed of hydrogen in its plasma state.

15. Chemical Equilibrium

CHAPTER HIGHLIGHTS & NOTES: KEY TERMS, PEOPLE, PLACES, CONCEPTS

Iodine	Iodine is a chemical element with symbol I and atomic number 53. The name is from Greek ??e?d?? ioeides, meaning violet or purple, due to the color of elemental iodine vapor. Iodine and its compounds are primarily used in nutrition, and industrially in the production of acetic acid and certain polymers. Iodine's relatively high atomic number, low toxicity, and ease of attachment to organic compounds have made it a part of many X-ray contrast materials in modern medicine.
Logarithm	The logarithm of a number is the exponent to which another fixed value, the base, must be raised to produce that number. For example, the logarithm of 1000 to base 10 is 3, because 10 to the power 3 is 1000: 1000 = 10?×?10?×?10 = 10^3. More generally, if $x = b^y$, then y is the logarithm of x to base b, and is written $y = \log_b(x)$, or $y = \log_b(b^y)$, so $\log_{10}(1000) = \log_{10}(10^3) = 3$. The logarithm to base 10 (b = 10) is called the common logarithm and has many applications in science and engineering. The natural logarithm has the irrational (transcendental) number e (˜ 2.718) as its base; its use is widespread in pure mathematics, especially calculus.
Concentration	In chemistry, concentration is the abundance of a constituent divided by the total volume of a mixture. Several types of mathematical description can be distinguished: mass concentration, molar concentration, number concentration, and volume concentration. The term concentration can be applied to any kind of chemical mixture, but most frequently it refers to solutes and solvents in solutions.
Reversible reaction	A reversible reaction is a chemical reaction that results in an equilibrium mixture of reactants and products. For a reaction involving two reactants and two products this can be expressed symbolically as $aA + bB \rightleftharpoons cC + dD$ A and B can react to form C and D or, in the reverse reaction, C and D can react to form A and B. This is distinct from reversible process in thermodynamics. The concentrations of reactants and products in an equilibrium mixture are determined by the analytical concentrations of the reagents (A and B or C and D) and the equilibrium constant, K. The magnitude of the equilibrium constant depends on the Gibbs free energy change for the reaction.
Equilibrium constant	For a general chemical equilibrium $\alpha A + \beta B ... \rightleftharpoons \rho R + \sigma S ...$ the thermodynamic equilibrium constant can be defined such that, at equilibrium, $K^\ominus = \frac{\{R\}^\rho \{S\}^\sigma ...}{\{A\}^\alpha \{B\}^\beta ...}$

where curly brackets denote the thermodynamic activities of the chemical species. The logarithm of this expression appears in the formula for the Gibbs free energy change for the reaction. If deviations from ideal behaviour are neglected, the activities may be replaced by concentrations, [A], and a concentration quotient, K_c.

Carbon	Carbon fiber, alternatively graphite fiber, carbon graphite or CF, is a material consisting of fibers about 5-10 μm in diameter and composed mostly of carbon atoms. The carbon atoms are bonded together in crystals that are more or less aligned parallel to the long axis of the fiber. The crystal alignment gives the fiber high strength-to-volume ratio (making it strong for its size).
Glycolipid	Glycolipids are lipids with a carbohydrate attached. Their role is to provide energy and also serve as markers for cellular recognition.
Phospholipid	Phospholipids are a class of lipids that are a major component of all cell membranes as they can form lipid bilayers. Most phospholipids contain a diglyceride, a phosphate group and a simple organic molecule such as choline; one exception to this rule is sphingomyelin, which is derived from sphingosine instead of glycerol. The first phospholipid identified as such in biological tissues was lecithin, or phosphatidylcholine, in the egg yolk, by Theodore Nicolas Gobley, a French chemist and pharmacist, in 1847. The structure of the phospholipid molecule generally consists of hydrophobic tails and a hydrophilic head.
Steroid	A steroid is a type of organic compound that contains a characteristic arrangement of four cycloalkane rings that are joined to each other. Examples of steroids include the dietary fat cholesterol, the sex hormones estradiol and testosterone and the anti-inflammatory drug dexamethasone. The core of steroids is composed of twenty carbon atoms bonded together that take the form of four fused rings: three cyclohexane rings (designated as rings A, B and C in the figure to the right) and one cyclopentane ring (the D ring).
Calcium	Calcium is the chemical element with symbol Ca and atomic number 20. Calcium is a soft gray alkaline earth metal, and is the fifth-most-abundant element by mass in the Earth's crust. Calcium is also the fifth-most-abundant dissolved ion in seawater by both molarity and mass, after sodium, chloride, magnesium, and sulfate. Calcium is essential for living organisms, in particular in cell physiology, where movement of the calcium ion Ca^{2+} into and out of the cytoplasm functions as a signal for many cellular processes.
Calcium oxide	Calcium oxide, commonly known as quicklime or burnt lime, is a widely used chemical compound. It is a white, caustic, alkaline crystalline solid at room temperature.

15. Chemical Equilibrium

CHAPTER HIGHLIGHTS & NOTES: KEY TERMS, PEOPLE, PLACES, CONCEPTS

Ideal gas

An ideal gas is a theoretical gas composed of a set of randomly moving, non-interacting point particles. The ideal gas concept is useful because it obeys the ideal gas law, a simplified equation of state, and is amenable to analysis under statistical mechanics.

At normal conditions such as standard temperature and pressure, most real gases behave qualitatively like an ideal gas.

Ideal gas law

The ideal gas law is the equation of state of a hypothetical ideal gas. It is a good approximation to the behaviour of many gases under many conditions, although it has several limitations. It was first stated by Émile Clapeyron in 1834 as a combination of Boyle's law and Charles's law.

Volume

In thermodynamics, the volume of a system is an important extensive parameter for describing its thermodynamic state. The specific volume, an intensive property, is the system's volume per unit of mass. Volume is a function of state and is interdependent with other thermodynamic properties such as pressure and temperature.

Hemoglobin

Hemoglobin; also spelled haemoglobin and abbreviated Hb or Hgb, is the iron-containing oxygen-transport metalloprotein in the red blood cells of all vertebrates as well as the tissues of some invertebrates. Hemoglobin in the blood carries oxygen from the respiratory organs (lungs or gills) to the rest of the body (i.e. the tissues) where it releases the oxygen to burn nutrients to provide energy to power the functions of the organism, and collects the resultant carbon dioxide to bring it back to the respiratory organs to be dispensed from the organism.

In mammals, the protein makes up about 97% of the red blood cells' dry content (by weight), and around 35% of the total content (including water).

Oxygen

Oxygen is a chemical element with symbol O and atomic number 8. It is a member of the chalcogen group on the periodic table and is a highly reactive nonmetallic element and oxidizing agent that readily forms compounds (notably oxides) with most elements. By mass, oxygen is the third-most abundant element in the universe, after hydrogen and helium At STP, two atoms of the element bind to form dioxygen, a diatomic gas that is colorless, odorless, and tasteless; with the formula O2.

Many major classes of organic molecules in living organisms, such as proteins, nucleic acids, carbohydrates, and fats, contain oxygen, as do the major inorganic compounds that are constituents of animal shells, teeth, and bone.

Excited state

Excitation is an elevation in energy level above an arbitrary baseline energy state. In physics there is a specific technical definition for energy level which is often associated with an atom being excited to an excited state.

Nitrite	The nitrite ion, which has the chemical formula NO_2^-, is a symmetric anion with equal N-O bond lengths and an O-N-O bond angle of approximately 120°. Upon protonation, the unstable weak acid nitrous acid is produced. Nitrite can be oxidized or reduced, with the product somewhat dependent on the oxidizing/reducing agent and its strength.
Nitrogen	Nitrogen, symbol N, is the chemical element of atomic number 7. At room temperature, it is a gas of diatomic molecules and is colorless and odorless. Nitrogen is a common element in the universe, estimated at about seventh in total abundance in our galaxy and the Solar System. On Earth, the element is primarily found as the free element; it forms about 80% of the Earth's atmosphere.
Molar solubility	Molar solubility is the number of moles of a substance that can be dissolved per liter of solution before the solution becomes saturated. It can be calculated from a substance's solubility product constant (K_{sp}) and stoichiometry. The units are mol/L, sometimes written as M
Silver chloride	Silver chloride is a chemical compound with the chemical formula AgCl. This white crystalline solid is well known for its low solubility in water (this behavior being reminiscent of the chlorides of Tl^+ and Pb^{2+}). Upon illumination or heating, silver chloride converts to silver (and chlorine), which is signaled by greyish or purplish coloration to some samples.
Hard water	Hard water is water that has high mineral content . Hard drinking water is generally not harmful to one's health, but can pose serious problems in industrial settings, where water hardness is monitored to avoid costly breakdowns in boilers, cooling towers, and other equipment that handles water. In domestic settings, hard water is often indicated by a lack of suds formation when soap is agitated in water, and by the formation of limescale in kettles and water heaters.
Carbon monoxide	Carbon monoxide is a colorless, odorless, and tasteless gas that is slightly less dense than air. It is toxic to humans and animals when encountered in higher concentrations, although it is also produced in normal animal metabolism in low quantities, and is thought to have some normal biological functions. In the atmosphere, it is spatially variable, short lived, having a role in the formation of ground-level ozone.
Catalyst	Catalysis is the increase rate of a chemical reaction due to the participation of a substance called a catalyst. Unlike other reagents in the chemical reaction, a catalyst is not consumed. With a catalyst, less free energy is required to reach the transition state, but the total free energy from reactants to products does not change.
Chlorofluorocarbon	A chlorofluorocarbon is an organic compound that contains only carbon, chlorine, and fluorine, produced as a volatile derivative of methane and ethane.

15. Chemical Equilibrium

CHAPTER HIGHLIGHTS & NOTES: KEY TERMS, PEOPLE, PLACES, CONCEPTS

They are also commonly known by the DuPont brand name Freon. The most common representative is dichlorodifluoromethane (R-12 or Freon-12).

Ozone — Ozone, or trioxygen, is an inorganic compound with the chemical formula O3(μ-O) (also written [O (μ-O)O] or O3). It is a pale blue gas with a distinctively pungent smell. It is an allotrope of oxygen that is much less stable than the diatomic allotrope O2, breaking down in the lower atmosphere to normal dioxygen.

Enzyme — Enzymes are large biological molecules responsible for the thousands of metabolic processes that sustain life. They are highly selective catalysts, greatly accelerating both the rate and specificity of metabolic reactions, from the digestion of food to the synthesis of DNA. Most enzymes are proteins, although some catalytic RNA molecules have been identified. Enzymes adopt a specific three-dimensional structure, and may employ organic (e.g. biotin) and inorganic (e.g. magnesium ion) cofactors to assist in catalysis.

CHAPTER QUIZ: KEY TERMS, PEOPLE, PLACES, CONCEPTS

1. A _________ exists once a reversible reaction ceases to change its ratio of reactants/products, but substances move between the chemicals at an equal rate, meaning there is no net change. It is a particular example of a system in a steady state. In thermodynamics a closed system is in thermo_________ when reactions occur at such rates that the composition of the mixture does not change with time.

   a. Binding constant
   b. Dynamic equilibrium
   c. Bromley equation
   d. Buffer solution

2. An _________ is a theoretical gas composed of a set of randomly moving, non-interacting point particles. The _________ concept is useful because it obeys the _________ law, a simplified equation of state, and is amenable to analysis under statistical mechanics.

   At normal conditions such as standard temperature and pressure, most real gases behave qualitatively like an _________.

   a. Bisulfide
   b. Buffer solution
   c. Ideal gas
   d. Carbonate alkalinity

3. . _________s are diagrams that show the bonding between atoms of a molecule and the lone pairs of electrons that may exist in the molecule. A _________ can be drawn for any covalently bonded molecule, as well as coordination compounds.

The _________ was named after Gilbert N

a. Lewis structure
b. covalent
c. Double bond
d. Formal charge

4. In chemistry, _________ is the abundance of a constituent divided by the total volume of a mixture. Several types of mathematical description can be distinguished: mass _________, molar _________, number _________, and volume _________. The term _________ can be applied to any kind of chemical mixture, but most frequently it refers to solutes and solvents in solutions.

a. Biomonitoring
b. Blank
c. Bradford protein assay
d. Concentration

5. _________ fiber, alternatively graphite fiber, _________ graphite or CF, is a material consisting of fibers about 5-10 μm in diameter and composed mostly of _________ atoms. The _________ atoms are bonded together in crystals that are more or less aligned parallel to the long axis of the fiber. The crystal alignment gives the fiber high strength-to-volume ratio (making it strong for its size).

a. Bamboo charcoal
b. Benzotriyne
c. Bilayer graphene
d. Carbon

ANSWER KEY
15. Chemical Equilibrium

1. b
2. c
3. a
4. d
5. d

---

16. Oxidation and Reduction

CHAPTER OUTLINE: KEY TERMS, PEOPLE, PLACES, CONCEPTS

Fuel cell

Oxygen

Oxidation

Combustion

Methane

Electron

Lewis structure

Lithium

Nonmetal

Oxidizing agent

Reducing agent

Oxidation state

Sulfur

Hydrogen peroxide

Sulfonic acid

Thiol

Half-reaction

Redox

Photosynthesis

Magnesium

Gold

16. Oxidation and Reduction

CHAPTER OUTLINE: KEY TERMS, PEOPLE, PLACES, CONCEPTS

- Dissociation
- Hydrochloric acid
- Nitric acid
- Oxide
- Anode
- Battery
- Cathode
- Current
- Electrochemical cell
- Galvanic cell
- Half-cell
- Salt bridge
- Platinum
- Sulfuric acid
- Electrolysis
- Electrolytic cell
- Electrolysis of water
- Corrosion
- Acetic acid
- Breathalyzer
- Radiation

16. Oxidation and Reduction

CHAPTER OUTLINE: KEY TERMS, PEOPLE, PLACES, CONCEPTS

- ________ Isotope
- ________ Absorption
- ________ Phosphorescence
- ________ Uranium
- ________ Atomic number
- ________ Curie
- ________ Curium
- ________ Polonium
- ________ Radium
- ________ Rutherford
- ________ Alpha decay
- ________ Ionization
- ________ Beta decay
- ________ Mass number
- ________ Electromagnetic radiation
- ________ Positron emission
- ________ Positron
- ________ Bismuth
- ________ Half-life
- ________ Scintillation counter
- ________ Radon

16. Oxidation and Reduction

CHAPTER OUTLINE: KEY TERMS, PEOPLE, PLACES, CONCEPTS

- Radiocarbon dating
- Barium
- Fermium
- Krypton
- Meitnerium
- Nuclear fission
- Boiling point
- Critical mass
- Einstein
- Nuclear power
- Nuclear fusion
- Deuterium
- Tritium

16. Oxidation and Reduction

CHAPTER HIGHLIGHTS & NOTES: KEY TERMS, PEOPLE, PLACES, CONCEPTS

Fuel cell

A fuel cell is a device that converts the chemical energy from a fuel into electricity through a chemical reaction with oxygen or another oxidizing agent. Hydrogen is the most common fuel, but hydrocarbons such as natural gas and alcohols like methanol are sometimes used. Fuel cells are different from batteries in that they require a constant source of fuel and oxygen/air to sustain the chemical reaction; however, fuel cells can produce electricity continually for as long as these inputs are supplied.

Oxygen

Oxygen is a chemical element with symbol O and atomic number 8. It is a member of the chalcogen group on the periodic table and is a highly reactive nonmetallic element and oxidizing agent that readily forms compounds (notably oxides) with most elements. By mass, oxygen is the third-most abundant element in the universe, after hydrogen and helium At STP, two atoms of the element bind to form dioxygen, a diatomic gas that is colorless, odorless, and tasteless; with the formula O2.

Many major classes of organic molecules in living organisms, such as proteins, nucleic acids, carbohydrates, and fats, contain oxygen, as do the major inorganic compounds that are constituents of animal shells, teeth, and bone.

Oxidation

Redox (reduction-oxidation) reactions include all chemical reactions in which atoms have their oxidation state changed; in general, redox reactions involve the transfer of electrons between species.

This can be either a simple redox process, such as the oxidation of carbon to yield carbon dioxide or the reduction of carbon by hydrogen to yield methane (CH_4), or a complex process such as the oxidation of glucose ($C_6H_{12}O_6$) in the human body through a series of complex electron transfer processes.

The term 'redox' comes from two concepts involved with electron transfer: reduction and oxidation.

Combustion

Combustion or burning is the sequence of exothermic chemical reactions between a fuel and an oxidant accompanied by the production of heat and conversion of chemical species. The release of heat can produce light in the form of either glowing or a flame.

In a complete combustion reaction, a compound reacts with an oxidizing element, such as oxygen or fluorine, and the products are compounds of each element in the fuel with the oxidizing element.

Methane

Methane is a chemical compound with the chemical formula CH4 (one atom of carbon and four atoms of hydrogen). It is the simplest alkane and the main component of natural gas. The relative abundance of methane makes it an attractive fuel.

Electron

The electron is a subatomic particle with a negative elementary electric charge.

Electrons belong to the first generation of the lepton particle family, and are generally thought to be elementary particles because they have no known components or substructure. The electron has a mass that is approximately 1/1836 that of the proton.

Lewis structure

Lewis structures are diagrams that show the bonding between atoms of a mo ecule and the lone pairs of electrons that may exist in the molecule. A Lewis structure can be drawn for any covalently bonded molecule, as well as coordination compounds. The Lewis structure was named after Gilbert N

Lithium

Lithium is a chemical element with symbol Li and atomic number 3. It is a soft silver-white metal belonging to the alkali metal group of chemical elements. Under standard conditions it is the lightest metal and the least dense solid element. Like all alkali metals, lithium is highly reactive and flammable.

Nonmetal

In chemistry, a nonmetal or non-metal is a chemical element which mostly lacks metallic attributes. Physically, nonmetals tend to be highly volatile (easily vaporised), have low elasticity, and are good insulators of heat and electricity; chemically, they tend to have high ionisation energy and electronegativity values, and gain or share electrons when they react with other elements or compounds. Seventeen elements are generally classified as nonmetals; most are gases (hydrogen, helium, nitrogen, oxygen, fluorine, neon, chlorine, argon, krypton, xenon and radon); one is a liquid (bromine); and a few are solids (carbon, phosphorus, sulfur, selenium, and iodine).

Oxidizing agent

An oxidizing agent is the element or compound in an oxidation-reduction (redox) reaction that accepts an electron from another species. Because the oxidizing agent is gaining electrons, it is said to have been reduced.

The oxidizing agent itself is reduced, as it is taking electrons onto itself, but the reactant is oxidized by having its electrons taken away by the oxidizing agent.

Reducing agent

A reducing agent is the element or compound in an oxidation-reduction reaction that donates an electron to another species. Because the reducing agent is losing electrons, we say it has been oxidized.

This means that there must be an 'oxidizer'; because if any chemical is an electron donor (reducer), another must be an electron recipient (oxidizer).

Oxidation state

The oxidation state, often called the oxidation number, is an indicator of the degree of oxidation of an atom in a chemical compound. The formal oxidation state is the hypothetical charge that an atom would have if all bonds to atoms of different elements were 100% ionic. Oxidation states are typically represented by integers, which can be positive, negative, or zero.

Sulfur

Sulfur or sulphur is a chemical element with symbol S and atomic number 16.

It is an abundant, multivalent non-metal. Under normal conditions, sulfur atoms form cyclic octatomic molecules with chemical formula S_8. Elemental sulfur is a bright yellow crystalline solid when at room temperature.

Hydrogen peroxide

Hydrogen peroxide is the simplest peroxide (a compound with an oxygen-oxygen single bond). It is also a strong oxidizer. Hydrogen peroxide is a clear liquid, slightly more viscous than water.

Sulfonic acid

A sulfonic acid refers to a member of the class of organosulfur compounds with the general formula $RS(=O)_2$-OH, where R is an organic alkyl or aryl group and the $S(=O)_2$-OH group a sulfonyl hydroxide. A sulfonic acid can be thought of as sulfuric acid with one hydroxyl group replaced by an organic substituent. The parent compound (with the organic substituent replaced by hydrogen) is the hypothetical compound sulfurous acid.

Thiol

In organic chemistry, a thiol is an organosulfur compound that contains a carbon-bonded sulfhydryl (-C-SH or R-SH) group (where R represents an alkane, alkene, or other carbon-containing group of atoms). Thiols are the sulfur analogue of alcohols (that is, sulfur takes the place of oxygen in the hydroxyl group of an alcohol), and the word is a portmanteau of 'thion' + 'alcohol', with the first word deriving from Greek ?e??? ('thion') = 'sulfur'. The -SH functional group itself is referred to as either a thiol group or a sulfhydryl group.

Half-reaction

A half reaction is either the oxidation or reduction reaction component of a redox reaction. A half reaction is obtained by considering the change in oxidation states of individual substances involved in the redox reaction.

Often, the concept of half-reactions is used to describe what occurs in an electrochemical cell, such as a Galvanic cell battery.

Redox

Redox reactions include all chemical reactions in which atoms have their oxidation state changed; redox reactions generally involve the transfer of electrons between species.

This can be either a simple redox process, such as the oxidation of carbon to yield carbon dioxide (CO2) or the reduction of carbon by hydrogen to yield methane (CH_4), or a complex process such as the oxidation of glucose ($C_6H_{12}O_6$) in the human body through a series of complex electron transfer processes.

The term 'redox' comes from two concepts involved with electron transfer: reduction and oxidation.

Photosynthesis

Photosynthesis is a process used by plants and other organisms to convert light energy, normally from the sun, into chemical energy that can be later released to fuel the organisms' activities. This chemical energy is stored in carbohydrate molecules, such as sugars, which are synthesized from carbon dioxide and water - hence the name photosynthesis, from the Greek f??, phos, 'light', and s???es??, synthesis, 'putting together'.

Magnesium

Magnesium is a chemical element with the symbol Mg and atomic number 12. Its common oxidation number is +2. It is an alkaline earth metal and the eighth most abundant element in the Earth's crust and ninth in the known universe as a whole. Magnesium is the fourth most common element in the Earth as a whole (behind iron, oxygen and silicon), making up 13% of the planet's mass and a large fraction of the planet's mantle. The relative abundance of magnesium is related to the fact that it easily builds up in supernova stars from a sequential addition of three helium nuclei to carbon (which in turn is made from three helium nuclei).

Gold

Gold is a chemical element with the symbol Au and atomic number 79. It is a dense, soft, malleable, and ductile metal with an attractive, bright yellow color and luster that is maintained without tarnishing in air or water. Chemically, gold is a transition metal and a group 11 element. It is one of the least reactive chemical elements, solid under standard conditions.

Dissociation

Dissociation in chemistry and biochemistry is a general process in which ionic compounds separate or split into smaller particles, ions, or radicals, usually in a reversible manner. For instance, when a Brønsted-Lowry acid is put in water, a covalent bond between an electronegative atom and a hydrogen atom is broken by heterolytic fission, which gives a proton and a negative ion. Dissociation is the opposite of association and recombination.

Hydrochloric acid

Hydrochloric acid is a clear, colorless, highly pungent solution of hydrogen chloride in water. It is a highly corrosive, strong mineral acid with many industrial uses. Hydrochloric acid is found naturally in gastric acid.

Nitric acid

Nitric acid, also known as aqua fortis and spirit of niter, is a highly corrosive strong mineral acid. The pure compound is colorless, but older samples tend to acquire a yellow cast due to decomposition into oxides of nitrogen and water. Most commercially available nitric acid has a concentration of 68%.

Oxide

An oxide is a chemical compound that contains at least one oxygen atom and one other element in its chemical formula. Metal oxides typically contain an anion of oxygen in the oxidation state of -2. Most of the Earth's crust consists of solid oxides, the result of elements being oxidized by the oxygen in air or in water. Hydrocarbon combustion affords the two principal carbon oxides: carbon monoxide and carbon dioxide.

Anode

An anode is an electrode through which electric current flows into a polarized electrical device. The direction of electric current is, by convention, opposite to the direction of electron flow. In other words, the electrons flow from the anode into, for example, an electrical circuit.

Battery

An electric battery is a device consisting of one or more electrochemical cells that convert stored chemical energy into electrical energy. Each battery consists of a negative electrode material, a positive electrode material, an electrolyte that allows ions to move between the electrodes, and terminals that allow current to flow out of the battery to perform work.

16. Oxidation and Reduction

CHAPTER HIGHLIGHTS & NOTES: KEY TERMS, PEOPLE, PLACES, CONCEPTS

Cathode

A cathode is an electrode through which electric current flows out of a polarized electrical device. The direction of electric current is, by convention, opposite to the direction of electron flow--thus, electrons are considered to flow toward the cathode electrode while current flows away from it. This convention is sometimes remembered using the mnemonic CCD for cathode current departs.

Current

A current in a fluid is the magnitude and direction of flow within that fluid. An air current presents the same properties specifically for a gaseous medium.

Types of fluid currents include•Boundary current•Current a current in a river or stream•Ocean current•Rip current•Subsurface currents•Turbidity current.

Electrochemical cell

An electrochemical cell is a device capable of either deriving electrical energy from chemical reactions, or facilitating chemical reactions through the introduction of electrical energy. A common example of an electrochemical cell is a standard 1.5-volt 'battery'. (Actually a single 'Galvanic cell'; a battery properly consists of multiple cells, connected in either parallel or series pattern).

Galvanic cell

A galvanic cell, or voltaic cell or Alessandro Volta respectively, is an electrochemical cell that derives electrical energy from spontaneous redox reactions taking place within the cell. It generally consists of two different metals connected by a salt bridge, or individual half-cells separated by a porous membrane.

Volta was the inventor of the voltaic pile, the first electrical battery.

Half-cell

A half-cell is a structure that contains a conductive electrode and a surrounding conductive electrolyte separated by a naturally occurring Helmholtz double layer. Chemical reactions within this layer momentarily pump electric charges between the electrode and the electrolyte, resulting in a potential difference between the electrode and the electrolyte. The typical anode reaction involves a metal atom in the electrode dissolved and transported as a positive ion across the double layer, causing the electrolyte to acquire a net positive charge while the electrode acquires a net negative charge.

Salt bridge

A salt bridge, in electrochemistry, is a laboratory device used to connect the oxidation and reduction half-cells of a galvanic cell, a type of electrochemical cell. Salt bridges usually come in two types: glass tube and filter paper.

Platinum

Platinum is a chemical element with the chemical symbol Pt and an atomic number of 78.

Its name is derived from the Spanish term platina, which is literally translated into 'little silver'. It is a dense, malleable, ductile, precious, gray-white transition metal.

Sulfuric acid

Sulfuric acid is a highly corrosive strong mineral acid with the molecular formula H_2SO_4. It is a pungent, colorless to slightly yellow viscous liquid which is soluble in water at all concentrations.

Electrolysis	In chemistry and manufacturing, electrolysis is a method of using a direct electric current to drive an otherwise non-spontaneous chemical reaction. Electrolysis is commercially highly important as a stage in the separation of elements from naturally occurring sources such as ores using an electrolytic cell.
Electrolytic cell	An electrolytic cell is an electrochemical cell that undergoes a redox reaction when electrical energy is applied. It is most often used to decompose chemical compounds, in a process called electrolysis--the Greek word lysis means to break up. When electrical energy is added to the system, the chemical energy is increased.
Electrolysis of water	Electrolysis of water is the decomposition of water into oxygen (O_2) and hydrogen gas (H_2) due to an electric current being passed through the water.
Corrosion	Corrosion is the gradual destruction of materials by chemical reaction with its environment. In the most common use of the word, this means electrochemical oxidation of metals in reaction with an oxidant such as oxygen. Rusting, the formation of iron oxides, is a well-known example of electrochemical corrosion.
Acetic acid	Acetic acid is an organic compound with the chemical formula CH_3COOH (also written as CH_3CO_2H or $C_2H_4O_2$). It is a colourless liquid that when undiluted is also called glacial acetic acid. Acetic acid is the main component of vinegar (apart from water; vinegar is roughly 8% acetic acid by volume), and has a distinctive sour taste and pungent smell.
Breathalyzer	A breathalyzer or breathalyser is a device for estimating blood alcohol content (BAC) from a breath sample. Breathalyzer is the brand name of a series of models made by one manufacturer of breath alcohol testing instruments (originally Stephenson Corporation, then Smith and Wesson, later sold to National Draeger), and is a registered trademark for such instruments. In Canada, a preliminary non-evidentiary screening device can be approved by Parliament as an approved screening device, and an evidentiary breath instrument can be similarly designated as an approved instrument.
Radiation	In physics, radiation is a process in which energetic particles or energetic waves travel through a vacuum, or through matter-containing media that are not required for their propagation. Waves of a mass filled medium itself, such as water waves or sound waves, are usually not considered to be forms of 'radiation' in this sense. Radiation can be classified as either ionizing or non-ionizing according to whether it ionizes or does not ionize ordinary chemical matter.
Isotope	Isotopes are variants of a particular chemical element such that, while all isotopes of a given element have the same number of protons in each atom, they differ in neutron number.

16. Oxidation and Reduction

	The term isotope is formed from the Greek roots isos (?s?? 'equal') and topos (t?p?? 'place'), meaning 'the same place'. Thus, different isotopes of a single element occupy the same position on the periodic table.
Absorption	In chemistry, absorption is a physical or chemical phenomenon or a process in which atoms, molecules, or ions enter some bulk phase - gas, liquid, or solid material. This is a different process from adsorption, since molecules undergoing absorption are taken up by the volume, not by the surface (as in the case for adsorption). A more general term is sorption, which covers absorption, adsorption, and ion exchange.
Phosphorescence	Phosphorescence is a specific type of photoluminescence related to fluorescence. Unlike fluorescence, a phosphorescent material does not immediately re-emit the radiation it absorbs. The slower time scales of the re-emission are associated with 'forbidden' energy state transitions in quantum mechanics.
Uranium	Uranium is a silvery-white metallic chemical element in the actinide series of the periodic table, with symbol U and atomic number 92. A uranium atom has 92 protons and 92 electrons, of which 6 are valence electrons. Uranium is weakly radioactive because all its isotopes are unstable. The most common isotopes of uranium are uranium-238 (which has 146 neutrons) and uranium-235 (which has 143 neutrons).
Atomic number	In chemistry and physics, the atomic number is the number of protons found in the nucleus of an atom and therefore identical to the charge number of the nucleus. It is conventionally represented by the symbol Z. The atomic number uniquely identifies a chemical element. In an atom of neutral charge, the atomic number is also equal to the number of electrons.
Curie	The curie is a non-SI unit of radioactivity the curie is widely used throughout the US government and industry. One curie is roughly the activity of 1 gram of the radium isotope ^{226}Ra, a substance studied by the Curies. The SI derived unit of radioactivity is the becquerel (Bq), which equates to one decay per second.
Curium	Curium is a transuranic radioactive chemical element with the symbol Cm and atomic number 96. This element of the actinide series was named after Marie Sklodowska-Curie and Pierre Curie - both were known for their research on radioactivity. Curium was first intentionally produced and identified in July 1944 by the group of Glenn T. Seaborg at the University of California, Berkeley. The discovery was kept secret and only released to the public in November 1945. Most curium is produced by bombarding uranium or plutonium with neutrons in nuclear reactors - one tonne of spent nuclear fuel contains about 20 grams of curium.

Polonium

Polonium is a chemical element with the symbol Po and atomic number 84, discovered in 1898 by Marie Curie and Pierre Curie. A rare and highly radioactive element with no stable isotopes, polonium is chemically similar to bismuth and tellurium, and it occurs in uranium ores. Applications of polonium are few, and include heaters in space probes, antistatic devices, and sources of neutrons and alpha particles.

Radium

Radium is a chemical element with symbol Ra and atomic number 88. Radium is an almost pure-white alkaline earth metal, but it readily oxidizes on exposure to air, becoming black in color. All isotopes of radium are highly radioactive, with the most stable isotope being radium-226, which has a half-life of 1601 years and decays into radon gas. Because of such instability, radium is luminescent, glowing a faint blue.

Rutherford

The rutherford is an obsolete unit of radioactivity, defined as the activity of a quantity of radioactive material in which one million nuclei decay per second. It is therefore equivalent to one megabecquerel. It was named after Ernest Rutherford.

Alpha decay

Alpha decay, or a-decay, is a type of radioactive decay in which an atomic nucleus emits an alpha particle and thereby transforms into an atom with a mass number 4 less and atomic number 2 less. For example, uranium-238 decaying through a-particle emission to form thorium-234 can be expressed as: ${}^{238}_{92}\mathrm{U} \rightarrow {}^{234}_{90}\mathrm{Th} + \alpha$

Because an alpha particle is the same as the nucleus of a helium-4 atom - consisting of two protons and two neutrons and thus having mass number 4 and atomic number 2 - this can also be written as: ${}^{238}_{92}\mathrm{U} \rightarrow {}^{234}_{90}\mathrm{Th} + {}^{4}_{2}\mathrm{He}$

Notice how, on either side of the nuclear equation, both the mass number and the atomic number are conserved: the mass number is 238 on the right side and (234 + 4) on the left side, and the atomic number is 92 on the right side and (90 + 2) on the left side.

The alpha particle also has a charge +2, but the charge is usually not written in nuclear equations, which describe nuclear reactions without considering the electrons.

Ionization

Ionization is the process by which an atom or a molecule acquires a negative or positive charge by gaining or losing electrons.

Beta decay

In nuclear physics, beta decay is a type of radioactive decay in which a beta particle (an electron or a positron) is emitted from an atomic nucleus. Beta decay is a process which allows the atom to obtain the optimal ratio of protons and neutrons.

Beta decay is mediated by the weak force.

16. Oxidation and Reduction

CHAPTER HIGHLIGHTS & NOTES: KEY TERMS, PEOPLE, PLACES, CONCEPTS

Mass number

The mass number, also called atomic mass number or nucleon number, is the total number of protons and neutrons (together known as nucleons) in an atomic nucleus. Because protons and neutrons both are baryons, the mass number A is identical with the baryon number B as of the nucleus as of the whole atom or ion. The mass number is different for each different isotope of a chemical element.

Electromagnetic radiation

Electromagnetic radiation is one of the fundamental phenomena of electromagnetism, behaving as waves propagating through space, and also as photon particles traveling through space, carrying radiant energy. In a vacuum, it propagates at a characteristic speed, the speed of light, normally in straight lines. EMR is emitted and absorbed by charged particles.

Positron emission

Positron emission or beta plus decay is a particular type of radioactive decay and a subtype of beta decay, in which a proton inside a radionuclide nucleus is converted into a neutron while releasing a positron and an electron neutrino (?$_e$). Positron emission is mediated by the weak force. The positron is a type of beta particle (ß$^+$), the other beta particle being the electron (ß$^-$) emitted from the ß$^-$ decay of a nucleus.

Positron

The positron or antielectron is the antiparticle or the antimatter counterpart of the electron. The positron has an electric charge of +1e, a spin of ½, and has the same mass as an electron. When a low-energy positron collides with a low-energy electron, annihilation occurs, resulting in the production of two or more gamma ray photons .

Bismuth

Bismuth is a chemical element with symbol Bi and atomic number 83. Bismuth, a pentavalent poor metal, chemically resembles arsenic and antimony. Elemental bismuth may occur naturally, although its sulfide and oxide form important commercial ores. The free element is 86% as dense as lead.

Half-life

Half-life is the amount of time required for a quantity to fall to half its value as measured at the beginning of the time period. While the term 'half-life' can be used to describe any quantity which follows an exponential decay, it is most often used within the context of nuclear physics and nuclear chemistry--that is, the time required, probabilistically, for half of the unstable, radioactive atoms in a sample to undergo radioactive decay.

The original term, dating to Ernest Rutherford's discovery of the principle in 1907, was 'half-life period', which was shortened to 'half-life' in the early 1950s.

Scintillation counter

A scintillation counter is an instrument for detecting and measuring ionizing radiation.

It consists of a scintillator which generates photons of light in response to incident radiation, a sensitive photomultiplier tube which converts the light to an electrical signal, and the necessary electronics to process the photomultiplier tube output.

Radon	Radon is a chemical element with symbol Rn and atomic number 86. It is a radioactive, colorless, odorless, tasteless noble gas, occurring naturally as an indirect decay product of uranium or thorium. Its most stable isotope, ^{222}Rn, has a half-life of 3.8 days. Radon is one of the densest substances that remains a gas under normal conditions.
Radiocarbon dating	Radiocarbon dating is a radiometric dating technique that uses the decay of carbon-14 (14C) to estimate the age of organic materials, such as wood and leather, up to about 58,000 to 62,000 years Before Present (BP, present defined as 1950). Carbon dating was presented to the world by Willard Libby in 1949, for which he was awarded the Nobel Prize in Chemistry. Since the introduction of carbon dating, the method has been used to date many items, including samples of the Dead Sea Scrolls, the Shroud of Turin, enough Egyptian artifacts to supply a chronology of Dynastic Egypt, and Ötzi the Iceman.
Barium	Barium is a chemical element with symbol Ba and atomic number 56. It is the fifth element in Group 2, a soft silvery metallic alkaline earth metal. Because of its high chemical reactivity barium is never found in nature as a free element. Its hydroxide was known in pre-modern history as baryta; this substance does not occur as a mineral, but can be prepared by heating barium carbonate.
Fermium	Fermium is a synthetic element with symbol Fm and atomic number 100. It is a member of the actinide series. It is the heaviest element that can be formed by neutron bombardment of lighter elements, and hence the last element that can be prepared in macroscopic quantities, although pure fermium metal has not yet been prepared. A total of 19 isotopes are known with ^{257}Fm being the longest-lived with a half-life of 100.5 days.
Krypton	Krypton is a chemical element with symbol Kr and atomic number 36. It is a member of group 18 (noble gases) elements. A colorless, odorless, tasteless noble gas, krypton occurs in trace amounts in the atmosphere, is isolated by fractionally distilling liquified air, and is often used with other rare gases in fluorescent lamps. Krypton is inert for most practical purposes.
Meitnerium	Meitnerium is a chemical element with symbol Mt and atomic number 109. It is an extremely radioactive synthetic element (an element not found in nature that can be created in a laboratory). The most stable known isotope, meitnerium-278, has a half-life of 7.6 seconds. The GSI Helmholtz Centre for Heavy Ion Research near Darmstadt, Germany, first created this element in 1982.
Nuclear fission	In nuclear physics and nuclear chemistry, nuclear fission is either a nuclear reaction or a radioactive decay process in which the nucleus of a particle splits into smaller parts . The fission process often produces free neutrons and photons (in the form of gamma rays), and releases a very large amount of energy even by the energetic standards of radioactive decay.

16. Oxidation and Reduction

CHAPTER HIGHLIGHTS & NOTES: KEY TERMS, PEOPLE, PLACES, CONCEPTS

Boiling point	The boiling point of a substance is the temperature at which the vapor pressure of the liquid equals the pressure surrounding the liquid and the liquid changes into a vapor. A liquid in a vacuum has a lower boiling point than when that liquid is at atmospheric pressure. A liquid at high-pressure has a higher boiling point than when that liquid is at atmospheric pressure.
Critical mass	A critical mass is the smallest amount of fissile material needed for a sustained nuclear chain reaction. The critical mass of a fissionable material depends upon its nuclear properties (specifically, the nuclear fission cross-section), its density, its shape, its enrichment, its purity, its temperature, and its surroundings. The concept is important in nuclear weapon design.
Einstein	An einstein is a unit defined as the energy in one mole of photons. Because energy is inversely proportional to wavelength, the unit is frequency dependent. This unit is not part of the International System of Units and is redundant with the joule.
Nuclear power	Nuclear power, or nuclear energy, is the use of exothermic nuclear processes, to generate useful heat and electricity. The term includes nuclear fission, nuclear decay and nuclear fusion. Presently the nuclear fission of elements in the actinide series of the periodic table produce the vast majority of nuclear energy in the direct service of humankind, with nuclear decay processes, primarily in the form of geothermal energy, and radioisotope thermoelectric generators, in niche uses making up the rest.
Nuclear fusion	In nuclear physics, nuclear fusion is a nuclear reaction in which two or more atomic nuclei collide at a very high speed and join to form a new type of atomic nucleus. During this process, matter is not conserved because some of the mass of the fusing nuclei is converted to photons (energy). Fusion is the process that powers active or 'main sequence' stars.
Deuterium	Deuterium is one of two stable isotopes of hydrogen. It has a natural abundance in Earth's oceans of about one atom in 6,420 of hydrogen. Thus deuterium accounts for approximately 0.0156% (or on a mass basis: 0.0312%) of all the naturally occurring hydrogen in the oceans, while the most common isotope (hydrogen-1 or protium) accounts for more than 99.98%.
Tritium	Tritium is a radioactive isotope of hydrogen. The nucleus of tritium contains one proton and two neutrons, whereas the nucleus of protium (by far the most abundant hydrogen isotope) contains one proton and no neutrons. Naturally occurring tritium is extremely rare on Earth, where trace amounts are formed by the interaction of the atmosphere with cosmic rays.

1. _________ is an organic compound with the chemical formula CH_3COOH (also written as CH_3CO_2H or $C_2H_4O_2$). It is a colourless liquid that when undiluted is also called glacial _________. _________ is the main component of vinegar (apart from water; vinegar is roughly 8% _________ by volume), and has a distinctive sour taste and pungent smell.

   a. Acetic acid
   b. Buffering agent
   c. Carbonate alkalinity
   d. Charlot equation

2. _________s are diagrams that show the bonding between atoms of a molecule and the lone pairs of electrons that may exist in the molecule. A _________ can be drawn for any covalently bonded molecule, as well as coordination compounds. The _________ was named after Gilbert N

   a. Bond energy
   b. covalent
   c. Lewis structure
   d. Formal charge

3. In chemistry and physics, the _________ is the number of protons found in the nucleus of an atom and therefore identical to the charge number of the nucleus. It is conventionally represented by the symbol Z. The _________ uniquely identifies a chemical element. In an atom of neutral charge, the _________ is also equal to the number of electrons.

   a. Atomic number
   b. Feshbach resonance
   c. Fine structure
   d. Free-fall atomic model

4. . _________, or a-decay, is a type of radioactive decay in which an atomic nucleus emits an alpha particle and thereby transforms into an atom with a mass number 4 less and atomic number 2 less. For example, uranium-238 decaying through a-particle emission to form thorium-234 can be expressed as: ${}^{238}_{92}\mathrm{U} \rightarrow {}^{234}_{90}\mathrm{Th} + \alpha$

   Because an alpha particle is the same as the nucleus of a helium-4 atom - consisting of two protons and two neutrons and thus having mass number 4 and atomic number 2 - this can also be written as: ${}^{238}_{92}\mathrm{U} \rightarrow {}^{234}_{90}\mathrm{Th} + {}^{4}_{2}\mathrm{He}$

   Notice how, on either side of the nuclear equation, both the mass number and the atomic number are conserved: the mass number is 238 on the right side and (234 + 4) on the left side, and the atomic number is 92 on the right side and (90 + 2) on the left side.

   The alpha particle also has a charge +2, but the charge is usually not written in nuclear equations which describe nuclear reactions without considering the electrons.

   a. Alpha decay

b. Compton scattering
c. Bohr model
d. Bohr magneton

5. A _________ is a device that converts the chemical energy from a fuel into electricity through a chemical reaction with oxygen or another oxidizing agent. Hydrogen is the most common fuel, but hydrocarbons such as natural gas and alcohols like methanol are sometimes used. _________s are different from batteries in that they require a constant source of fuel and oxygen/air to sustain the chemical reaction; however, _________s can produce electricity continually for as long as these inputs are supplied.

   a. Fuel cell
   b. Bernard S. Baker
   c. Bloom Energy Server
   d. Direct borohydride fuel cell

ANSWER KEY
16. Oxidation and Reduction

1. a
2. c
3. a
4. a
5. a

CHAPTER OUTLINE: KEY TERMS, PEOPLE, PLACES, CONCEPTS

- Benzyl acetate
- Organic chemistry
- Molecule
- Carbon
- Carbon dioxide
- Cinnamaldehyde
- Lewis structure
- Triethylamine
- Inorganic compound
- Organic compound
- Vanillin
- Urea
- Hydrocarbon
- Alkane
- Carbon monoxide
- Fossil fuel
- Ozone
- Combustion
- Dioxide
- Propane
- Boiling point

17. Radioactivity and Nuclear Chemistry 61018 Organic Chemistry

CHAPTER OUTLINE: KEY TERMS, PEOPLE, PLACES, CONCEPTS

______ Decane

______ Hexane

______ Isobutane

______ Isomer

______ Substituent

______ Acetylene

______ Alkene

______ Alkyne

______ Unsaturated hydrocarbon

______ Oxygen

______ Addition reaction

______ Chloride ion

______ Chloroethane

______ Chloromethane

______ Ethane

______ Methane

______ Substitution reaction

______ Chlorine

______ Hydrogenation

______ Aromatic hydrocarbon

______ Benzene

CHAPTER OUTLINE: KEY TERMS, PEOPLE, PLACES, CONCEPTS

Propene

Vegetable oil

Bromobenzene

Chlorobenzene

Ethylbenzene

Phenol

Phenyl group

Alcohol

Functional group

Isopropyl alcohol

Methanol

Ethanol

Diethyl ether

Dimethyl ether

Ether

Rubbing alcohol

Alcoholic beverage

Aldehyde

Ketone

Acetone

Benzaldehyde

17. Radioactivity and Nuclear Chemistry 61018 Organic Chemistry

CHAPTER OUTLINE: KEY TERMS, PEOPLE, PLACES, CONCEPTS

- Formaldehyde
- 2-Heptanone
- Carboxylic acid
- Carvone
- Ionone
- Acetic acid
- Oxidation
- Citric acid
- Formic acid
- Lactic acid
- Acetylsalicylic acid
- Amine
- Aspirin
- Putrescine
- Trimethylamine
- Monomer
- Polyethylene
- Polymer
- Adipic acid
- Condensation polymer
- Copolymer

CHAPTER OUTLINE: KEY TERMS, PEOPLE, PLACES, CONCEPTS

	Hexamethylenediamine
	Dimer
	Kevlar

CHAPTER HIGHLIGHTS & NOTES: KEY TERMS, PEOPLE, PLACES, CONCEPTS

Benzyl acetate	Benzyl acetate is an organic compound with the molecular formula $C_9H_{10}O_2$. It is the ester formed by condensation of benzyl alcohol and acetic acid. Benzyl acetate is found naturally in many flowers.
Organic chemistry	Organic chemistry is a chemistry subdiscipline involving the scientific study of the structure, properties, and reactions of organic compounds and organic materials, i.e., matter in its various forms that contain carbon atoms. Study of structure includes using spectroscopy and other physical and chemical methods to determine the chemical composition and constitution of organic compounds and materials. Study of properties includes both physical properties and chemical properties, and uses similar methods as well as methods to evaluate chemical reactivity, with the aim to understand the behavior of the organic matter in its pure form (when possible), but also in solutions, mixtures, and fabricated forms.
Molecule	A molecule is an electrically neutral group of two or more atoms held together by chemical bonds. Molecules are distinguished from ions by their lack of electrical charge. However, in quantum physics, organic chemistry, and biochemistry, the term molecule is often used less strictly, also being applied to polyatomic ions.
Carbon	Carbon fiber, alternatively graphite fiber, carbon graphite or CF, is a material consisting of fibers about 5-10 μm in diameter and composed mostly of carbon atoms. The carbon atoms are bonded together in crystals that are more or less aligned parallel to the long axis of the fiber. The crystal alignment gives the fiber high strength-to-volume ratio (making it strong for its size).
Carbon dioxide	Carbon dioxide is a naturally occurring chemical compound composed of two oxygen atoms each covalently double bonded to a single carbon atom. It is a gas at standard temperature and pressure and exists in Earth's atmosphere in this state, as a trace gas at a concentration of 0.039 per cent by volume.

17. Radioactivity and Nuclear Chemistry 61018 Organic Chemistry

CHAPTER HIGHLIGHTS & NOTES: KEY TERMS, PEOPLE, PLACES, CONCEPTS

Cinnamaldehyde	Cinnamaldehyde is the organic compound that gives cinnamon its flavor and odor. This pale yellow, viscous liquid occurs naturally in the bark of cinnamon trees and other species of the genus Cinnamomum. The essential oil of cinnamon bark is about 90% cinnamaldehyde.
Lewis structure	Lewis structures are diagrams that show the bonding between atoms of a molecule and the lone pairs of electrons that may exist in the molecule. A Lewis structure can be drawn for any covalently bonded molecule, as well as coordination compounds. The Lewis structure was named after Gilbert N
Triethylamine	Triethylamine is the chemical compound with the formula N_3, commonly abbreviated Et_3N. It is also abbreviated TEA, yet this abbreviation must be used carefully to avoid confusion with triethanolamine or tetraethylammonium, for which TEA is also a common abbreviation. It is a colourless volatile liquid with a strong fishy odor reminiscent of ammonia and is also the smell of the hawthorn plant. Like diisopropylethylamine (Hünig's base), triethylamine is commonly encountered in organic synthesis.
Inorganic compound	Inorganic compounds are those that lack carbon and hydrogen atoms. Inorganic compounds are traditionally viewed as being synthesized by the agency of geological systems. In contrast, organic compounds are found in biological systems.
Organic compound	An organic compound is any member of a large class of gaseous, liquid, or solid chemical compounds whose molecules contain carbon. For historical reasons discussed below, a few types of carbon-containing compounds such as carbides, carbonates, simple oxides of carbon (such as CO and CO_2), and cyanides are considered inorganic. The distinction between 'organic' and 'inorganic' carbon compounds, while 'useful in organizing the vast subject of chemistry... is somewhat arbitrary'.
Vanillin	Vanillin is a phenolic aldehyde, which is an organic compound with the molecular formula $C_8H_8O_3$. Its functional groups include aldehyde, ether, and phenol. It is the primary component of the extract of the vanilla bean.
Urea	Urea or carbamide is an organic compound with the chemical formula CO_2. The molecule has two --NH_2 groups joined by a carbonyl (C=O) functional group. Urea serves an important role in the metabolism of nitrogen-containing compounds by animals and is the main nitrogen-containing substance in the urine of mammals.
Hydrocarbon	In organic chemistry, a hydrocarbon is an organic compound consisting entirely of hydrogen and carbon. Hydrocarbons from which one hydrogen atom has been removed are functional groups, called hydrocarbyls. Aromatic hydrocarbons (arenes), alkanes, alkenes, cycloalkanes and alkyne-based compounds are different types of hydrocarbons.

Alkane	In organic chemistry, an alkane, or paraffin, is a saturated hydrocarbon. Alkanes consist only of hydrogen and carbon atoms, all bonds are single bonds, and the carbon atoms are not joined in cyclic structures but instead form an open chain. They have the general chemical formula C_nH_{2n+2}.
Carbon monoxide	Carbon monoxide is a colorless, odorless, and tasteless gas that is slightly less dense than air. It is toxic to humans and animals when encountered in higher concentrations, although it is also produced in normal animal metabolism in low quantities, and is thought to have some normal biological functions. In the atmosphere, it is spatially variable, short lived, having a role in the formation of ground-level ozone.
Fossil fuel	Fossil fuels are fuels formed by natural processes such as anaerobic decomposition of buried dead organisms. The age of the organisms and their resulting fossil fuels is typically millions of years, and sometimes exceeds 650 million years. Fossil fuels contain high percentages of carbon and include coal, petroleum, and natural gas.
Ozone	Ozone, or trioxygen, is an inorganic compound with the chemical formula O3(μ-O) (also written [O (μ-O)O] or O3). It is a pale blue gas with a distinctively pungent smell. It is an allotrope of oxygen that is much less stable than the diatomic allotrope O2, breaking down in the lower atmosphere to normal dioxygen.
Combustion	Combustion or burning is the sequence of exothermic chemical reactions between a fuel and an oxidant accompanied by the production of heat and conversion of chemical species. The release of heat can produce light in the form of either glowing or a flame. In a complete combustion reaction, a compound reacts with an oxidizing element, such as oxygen or fluorine, and the products are compounds of each element in the fuel with the oxidizing element.
Dioxide	An oxide is a chemical compound that contains at least one oxygen atom and one other element in its chemical formula. Metal oxides typically contain an anion of oxygen in the oxidation state of -2. Most of the Earth's crust consists of solid oxides, the result of elements being oxidized by the oxygen in air or in water. Hydrocarbon combustion affords the two principal carbon oxides: carbon monoxide and carbon dioxide.
Propane	Propane is a three-carbon alkane with the molecular formula C3H8, normally a gas, but compressible to a transportable liquid. A by-product of natural gas processing and petroleum refining, it is commonly used as a fuel for engines, oxy-gas torches, barbecues, portable stoves, and residential central heating. Propane is one of a group of liquefied petroleum gases.
Boiling point	The boiling point of a substance is the temperature at which the vapor pressure of the liquid equals the pressure surrounding the liquid and the liquid changes into a vapor. A liquid in a vacuum has a lower boiling point than when that liquid is at atmospheric pressure.

17. Radioactivity and Nuclear Chemistry 61018 Organic Chemistry

CHAPTER HIGHLIGHTS & NOTES: KEY TERMS, PEOPLE, PLACES, CONCEPTS

Decane	Decane is an alkane hydrocarbon with the chemical formula $C_{10}H_{22}$ with 75 structural isomers. These isomers are flammable liquids. Decane is a component of gasoline (petrol).
Hexane	Hexane is an alkane of six carbon atoms, with the chemical formula C_6H_{14}. The term may refer to any of the five structural isomers with that formula, or to a mixture of them. In IUPAC nomenclature, however, hexane is the unbranched isomer (n-hexane); the other four structures are named as methylated derivatives of pentane and butane.
Isobutane	Isobutane, also known as methylpropane, is an isomer of butane. It is the simplest alkane with a tertiary carbon. Concerns with depletion of the ozone layer by freon gases have led to increased use of isobutane as a gas for refrigeration systems, especially in domestic refrigerators and freezers, and as a propellant in aerosol sprays.
Isomer	In chemistry, isomers (; from Greek ?s?µe???, isomerès; isos = 'equal', méros = 'part') are molecules with the same molecular formula but different chemical structures. That is, isomers contain the same number of atoms of each element, but have different arrangements of their atoms in space. Isomers do not necessarily share similar properties, unless they also have the same functional groups.
Substituent	In organic chemistry and biochemistry, a substituent is an atom or group of atoms substituted in place of a hydrogen atom on the parent chain of a hydrocarbon. The terms substituent, side-chain, group, branch, or pendant group are used almost interchangeably to describe branches from a parent structure, though certain distinctions are made in the context of polymer chemistry. In polymers, side chains extend from a backbone structure.
Acetylene	Acetylene is the chemical compound with the formula C_2H_2. It is a hydrocarbon and the simplest alkyne. This colorless gas is widely used as a fuel and a chemical building block.
Alkene	In organic chemistry, an alkene, olefin, or olefine is an unsaturated chemical compound containing at least one carbon-carbon double bond. The simplest acyclic alkenes, with only one double bond and no other functional groups, known as mono-enes, form a homologous series of hydrocarbons with the general formula C_nH_{2n}. They have two hydrogen atoms less than the corresponding alkane (with the same number of carbon atoms).
Alkyne	In organic chemistry, an alkyne is an unsaturated hydrocarbon which has at least one carbon--carbon triple bond between two carbon atoms. The simplest acyclic alkynes with only one triple bond and no other functional groups form a homologous series with the general chemical formula C_nH_{2n-2}. Alkynes are traditionally known as acetylenes, although the name acetylene also refers specifically to C_2H_2, known formally as ethyne using IUPAC nomenclature.

Unsaturated hydrocarbon	Unsaturated hydrocarbons are hydrocarbons that have double or triple covalent bonds between adjacent carbon atoms. Those with at least one carbon to carbon double bond are called alkenes and those with at least one carbon to carbon triple bond are called alkynes. The position of the double or triple bond is shown by a number written either at the start of the name, or just before the -ene or -yne suffix (e.g. pent-2-ene and 2-butyne).
Oxygen	Oxygen is a chemical element with symbol O and atomic number 8. It is a member of the chalcogen group on the periodic table and is a highly reactive nonmetallic element and oxidizing agent that readily forms compounds (notably oxides) with most elements. By mass, oxygen is the third-most abundant element in the universe, after hydrogen and helium At STP, two atoms of the element bind to form dioxygen, a diatomic gas that is colorless, odorless, and tasteless; with the formula O2. Many major classes of organic molecules in living organisms, such as proteins, nucleic acids, carbohydrates, and fats, contain oxygen, as do the major inorganic compounds that are constituents of animal shells, teeth, and bone.
Addition reaction	An addition reaction, in organic chemistry, is in its simplest terms an organic reaction where two or more molecules combine to form a larger one. Addition reactions are limited to chemical compounds that have multiple bonds, such as molecules with carbon-carbon double bonds, or with triple bonds (alkynes). Molecules containing carbon--hetero double bonds like carbonyl (C=O) groups, or imine (C=N) groups, can undergo addition as they too have double bond character.
Chloride ion	The chloride ion is the anion Cl^-. It is formed when the element chlorine (a halogen) gains an electron or when a compound such as hydrogen chloride is dissolved in water or other polar solvents. Chlorides salts such as sodium chloride are often very soluble in water.
Chloroethane	Chloroethane or monochloroethane, commonly known by its old name ethyl chloride, is a chemical compound with chemical formula C2H5Cl, once widely used in producing tetraethyllead, a gasoline additive. It is a colorless, flammable gas or refrigerated liquid with a faintly sweet odor.
Chloromethane	Chloromethane, also called methyl chloride, R-40 or HCC 40, is a chemical compound of the group of organic compounds called haloalkanes. It was once widely used as a refrigerant. It is a colorless extremely flammable gas with a mildly sweet odor, which is, however, detected at possibly toxic levels.
Ethane	Ethane is a chemical compound with chemical formula C_2H_6. At standard temperature and pressure, ethane is a colorless, odorless gas. Ethane is isolated on an industrial scale from natural gas, and as a byproduct of petroleum refining.

CHAPTER HIGHLIGHTS & NOTES: KEY TERMS, PEOPLE, PLACES, CONCEPTS

Methane	Methane is a chemical compound with the chemical formula CH4 (one atom of carbon and four atoms of hydrogen). It is the simplest alkane and the main component of natural gas. The relative abundance of methane makes it an attractive fuel.
Substitution reaction	Substitution reaction is also known as single displacement reaction and single replacement reaction. In a substitution reaction, a functional group in a particular chemical compound is replaced by another group. In organic chemistry, the electrophilic and nucleophilic substitution reactions are of prime importance.
Chlorine	Chlorine is a chemical element with symbol Cl and atomic number 17. Chlorine is in the halogen group (17) and is the second lightest halogen after fluorine. The element is a yellow-green gas under standard conditions, where it forms diatomic molecules. It has the highest electron affinity and the fourth highest electronegativity of all the reactive elements; for this reason, chlorine is a strong oxidizing agent.
Hydrogenation	Hydrogenation - to treat with hydrogen - is a chemical reaction between molecular hydrogen and another compound or element, usually in the presence of a catalyst. The process is commonly employed to reduce or saturate organic compounds. Hydrogenation typically constitutes the addition of pairs of hydrogen atoms to a molecule, generally an alkene.
Aromatic hydrocarbon	An aromatic hydrocarbon or arene is a hydrocarbon with alternating double and single bonds between carbon atoms forming rings. The term 'aromatic' was assigned before the physical mechanism determining aromaticity was discovered, and was derived from the fact that many of the compounds have a sweet scent. The configuration of six carbon atoms in aromatic compounds is known as a benzene ring, after the simplest possible such hydrocarbon, benzene.
Benzene	Benzene is an organic chemical compound with the molecular formula C_6H_6. Its molecule is composed of 6 carbon atoms joined in a ring, with 1 hydrogen atom attached to each carbon atom. Because its molecules contain only carbon and hydrogen atoms, benzene is classed as a hydrocarbon.
Propene	Propene, also known as propylene or methylethylene, is an unsaturated organic compound having the chemical formula C_3H_6. It has one double bond, and is the second simplest member of the alkene class of hydrocarbons.
Vegetable oil	A vegetable oil is a triglyceride extracted from a plant. Such oils have been part of human culture for millennia. The term 'vegetable oil' can be narrowly defined as referring only to substances that are liquid at room temperature, or broadly defined without regard to a substance's state of matter at a given temperature.
Bromobenzene	Bromobenzene is an aryl halide, C_6H_5Br, which can be formed by electrophilic aromatic substitution of benzene using bromine. It is a clear, colourless or pale yellow liquid.

Chlorobenzene	Chlorobenzene is an aromatic organic compound with the chemical formula C_6H_5Cl. This colorless, flammable liquid is a common solvent and a widely used intermediate in the manufacture of other chemicals.
Ethylbenzene	Ethylbenzene is an organic compound with the formula $C_6H_5CH_2CH_3$. It is a highly flammable, colorless liquid with an odor similar to that of gasoline. This monocyclic aromatic hydrocarbon is important in the petrochemical industry as an intermediate in the production of styrene, the precursor to polystyrene, a common plastic material.
Phenol	Phenol -- also known as carbolic acid -- is an aromatic organic compound with the molecular formula C_6H_5OH. It is a white crystalline solid that is volatile. The molecule consists of a phenyl group ($-C_6H_5$) bonded to a hydroxyl group (-OH). It is mildly acidic, but requires careful handling due to its propensity to cause burns.
Phenyl group	In organic chemistry, the phenyl group or phenyl ring is a cyclic group of atoms with the formula C_6H_5. Phenyl groups are closely related to benzene. Phenyl groups have six carbon atoms bonded together in a hexagonal planar ring, five of which are bonded to individual hydrogen atoms, with the remaining carbon bonded to a substituent.
Alcohol	In chemistry, an alcohol is an organic compound in which the hydroxyl functional group is bound to a carbon atom. In particular, this carbon center should be saturated, having single bonds to three other atoms. An important class of alcohols are the simple acyclic alcohols, the general formula for which is $C_nH_{2n+1}OH$. Of those, ethanol (C_2H_5OH) is the type of alcohol found in alcoholic beverages, and in common speech the word alcohol refers specifically to ethanol.
Functional group	In organic chemistry, functional groups are lexicon-specific groups of atoms or bonds within molecules that are responsible for the characteristic chemical reactions of those molecules. The same functional group will undergo the same or similar chemical reaction(s) regardless of the size of the molecule it is a part of. However, its relative reactivity can be modified by nearby functional groups.
Isopropyl alcohol	Isopropyl alcohol is a common name for a chemical compound with the molecular formula C_3H_8O or C_3H_7OH. It is a colorless, flammable chemical compound with a strong odor. It is the simplest example of a secondary alcohol, where the alcohol carbon atom is attached to two other carbon atoms sometimes shown as $(CH_3)_2CHOH$. It is a structural isomer of propanol. Isopropyl alcohol is denatured for certain uses, in which case the NFPA 704 rating is changed to 2,3,1
Methanol	Methanol, also known as methyl alcohol, wood alcohol, wood naphtha or wood spirits, is a chemical with the formula CH_3OH .

	Methanol acquired the name 'wood alcohol' because it was once produced chiefly as a byproduct of the destructive distillation of wood. Modern methanol is produced in a catalytic industrial process directly from carbon monoxide, carbon dioxide, and hydrogen.
Ethanol	Ethanol, also called ethyl alcohol, pure alcohol, grain alcohol, or drinking alcohol, is a volatile, flammable, colorless liquid with the structural formula CH_3CH_2OH, often abbreviated as C_2H_5OH or C_2H_6O. A psychoactive drug and one of the oldest recreational drugs, ethanol can cause alcohol intoxication when consumed. Best known as the type of alcohol found in alcoholic beverages, it is also used in thermometers, as a solvent, and as a fuel. In common usage, it is often referred to simply as alcohol or spirits.
Diethyl ether	Diethyl ether, also known as ethyl ether, sulfuric ether, simply ether, or ethoxyethane, is an organic compound in the ether class with the formula 2O. It is a colorless, highly volatile flammable liquid. It is commonly used as a solvent and was once used as a general anesthetic.
Dimethyl ether	Dimethyl ether, also known as methoxymethane, is the organic compound with the formula CH3OCH3. The simplest ether, it is a colourless gas that is a useful precursor to other organic compounds and an aerosol propellant.
Ether	Ethers are a class of organic compounds that contain an ether group -- an oxygen atom connected to two alkyl or aryl groups -- of general formula R-O-R'. A typical example is the solvent and anesthetic diethyl ether, commonly referred to simply as 'ether' (CH_3-CH_2-O-CH_2-CH_3). Ethers are common in organic chemistry and pervasive in biochemistry, as they are common linkages in carbohydrates and lignin.
Rubbing alcohol	Rubbing alcohol, USP / Surgical spirit, B.P. is a liquid prepared and used primarily for topical application. It is prepared from a special denatured alcohol solution and contains approximately 70 percent by volume of pure, concentrated ethanol (ethyl alcohol) or isopropyl alcohol (isopropanol). Individual manufacturers can use their own 'formulation standards' in which the ethanol content usually ranges from 70-99% v/v. In Ireland and the UK, the equivalent skin preparation is surgical spirit, which is always an ethyl alcohol-isopropyl alcohol mixture.
Alcoholic beverage	An alcoholic beverage is a drink that contains ethanol. Alcoholic beverages are divided into three general classes for taxation and regulation of production: beers, wines, and spirits (distilled beverages). They are legally consumed in most countries around the world.
Aldehyde	An aldehyde is an organic compound containing a formyl group. This functional group, with the structure R-CHO, consists of a carbonyl center (a carbon double bonded to oxygen) bonded to hydrogen and an R group, which is any generic alkyl or side chain. The group without R is called the aldehyde group or formyl group.

Ketone	In chemistry, a ketone is an organic compound with the structure RC(=O)R', where R and R' can be a variety of carbon-containing substituents. Ketones feature a carbonyl group (C=O) bonded to two other carbon atoms. Many ketones are known and many are of great importance in industry and in biology.
Acetone	Acetone is the organic compound with the formula $(CH_3)_2CO$. It is a colorless, mobile, flammable liquid, and is the simplest ketone. Acetone is miscible with water and serves as an important solvent in its own right, typically for cleaning purposes in the laboratory. About 6.7 million tonnes were produced worldwide in 2010, mainly for use as a solvent and production of methyl methacrylate and bisphenol A. It is a common building block in organic chemistry.
Benzaldehyde	Benzaldehyde is an organic compound consisting of a benzene ring with a formyl substituent. It is the simplest aromatic aldehyde and one of the most industrially useful. This colorless liquid has a characteristic pleasant almond-like odor.
Formaldehyde	Formaldehyde is an organic compound with the formula CH_2O or HCHO. It is the simplest aldehyde, hence its systematic name methanal. The common name of the substance comes from its similarity and relation to formic acid. A gas at room temperature, formaldehyde is colorless and has a characteristic pungent, irritating odor.
2-Heptanone	2-Heptanone, or methyl n-amyl ketone, is a ketone with the molecular formula $C_7H_{14}O$. It is a colorless, water-white liquid with a banana-like, fruity odor. 2-Heptanone is listed by the FDA as a 'food additive permitted for direct addition to food for human consumption' (21 CFR 172.515), and it occurs naturally in certain foods (e.g., beer, white bread, butter, various cheeses and potato chips). The mechanism of action of 2-heptanone as a pheromone at odorant receptors in rodents has been investigated.
Carboxylic acid	A carboxylic acid is an organic acid characterized by the presence of at least one carboxyl group. The general formula of a carboxylic acid is R-COOH, where R is some monovalent functional group. A carboxyl group (or carboxy) is a functional group consisting of a carbonyl (RR'C=O) and a hydroxyl (R-O-H), which has the formula -C(=O)OH, usually written as -COOH or $-CO_2H$. Carboxylic acids are Brønsted-Lowry acids because they are proton (H^+) donors.

17. Radioactivity and Nuclear Chemistry 61018 Organic Chemistry

CHAPTER HIGHLIGHTS & NOTES: KEY TERMS, PEOPLE, PLACES, CONCEPTS

Carvone	Carvone is a member of a family of chemicals called terpenoids. Carvone is found naturally in many essential oils, but is most abundant in the oils from seeds of caraway (Carum carvi) and dill.
Ionone	The ionones are a series of closely related chemical substances that are part of a group of compounds known as rose ketones, which also includes damascones and damascenones. Ionones are aroma compounds found in a variety of essential oils, including rose oil. beta-Ionone is a significant contributor to the aroma of roses, despite its relatively low concentration, and is an important fragrance chemical used in perfumery.
Acetic acid	Acetic acid is an organic compound with the chemical formula CH_3COOH (also written as CH_3CO_2H or $C_2H_4O_2$). It is a colourless liquid that when undiluted is also called glacial acetic acid. Acetic acid is the main component of vinegar (apart from water; vinegar is roughly 8% acetic acid by volume), and has a distinctive sour taste and pungent smell.
Oxidation	Redox (reduction-oxidation) reactions include all chemical reactions in which atoms have their oxidation state changed; in general, redox reactions involve the transfer of electrons between species. This can be either a simple redox process, such as the oxidation of carbon to yield carbon dioxide or the reduction of carbon by hydrogen to yield methane (CH_4), or a complex process such as the oxidation of glucose ($C_6H_{12}O_6$) in the human body through a series of complex electron transfer processes. The term 'redox' comes from two concepts involved with electron transfer: reduction and oxidation.
Citric acid	Citric acid is a weak organic acid with the formula $C_6H_8O_7$. It is a natural preservative/conservative and is also used to add an acidic or sour taste to foods and drinks. In biochemistry, the conjugate base of citric acid, citrate, is important as an intermediate in the citric acid cycle, which occurs in the metabolism of all aerobic organisms.
Formic acid	Formic acid is the simplest carboxylic acid. Its chemical formula is HCOOH or HCO_2H. It is an important intermediate in chemical synthesis and occurs naturally, most notably in ant venom. In fact, its name comes from the Latin word for ant, formica, referring to its early isolation by the distillation of ant bodies.
Lactic acid	Lactic acid, also known as milk acid, is a chemical compound that plays a role in various biochemical processes and was first isolated in 1780 by the Swedish chemist Carl Wilhelm Scheele. Lactic acid is a carboxylic acid with the chemical formula $C_3H_6O_3$. It has a hydroxyl group adjacent to the carboxyl group, making it an alpha hydroxy acid (AHA).
Acetylsalicylic acid	Aspirin, also known as acetylsalicylic acid (INN (?--?l--i-

	-ik) ASA), is a salicylate drug, often used as an analgesic to relieve minor aches and pains, as an antipyretic to reduce fever, and as an anti-inflammatory medication. The active ingredient of Aspirin was first discovered from the bark of the willow tree in 1763 by Edward Stone of Wadham College, Oxford University. He had discovered salicylic acid, the active metabolite of aspirin.
Amine	Amines are organic compounds and functional groups that contain a basic nitrogen atom with a lone pair. Amines are derivatives of ammonia, wherein one or more hydrogen atoms have been replaced by a substituent such as an alkyl or aryl group. Important amines include amino acids, biogenic amines, trimethylamine, and aniline; see Category:Amines for a list of amines.
Aspirin	Aspirin, also known as acetylsalicylic acid (INN (?--?l--i--ik) ASA), is a salicylate drug, often used as an analgesic to relieve minor aches and pains, as an antipyretic to reduce fever, and as an anti-inflammatory medication. Aspirin was first isolated by Felix Hoffmann, a chemist with the German company Bayer in 1897. Salicylic acid, the main metabolite of aspirin, is an integral part of human and animal metabolism.
Putrescine	Putrescine, or tetramethylenediamine, is a foul-smelling organic chemical compound $NH_{24}NH_2$ (1,4 -diaminobutane or butanediamine) that is related to cadaverine; both are produced by the breakdown of amino acids in living and dead organisms and both are toxic in large doses. The two compounds are largely responsible for the foul odor of putrefying flesh, but also contribute to the odor of such processes as bad breath and bacterial vaginosis. They are also found in semen and some microalgae, together with related molecules like spermine and spermidine.
Trimethylamine	Trimethylamine is an organic compound with the formula N_3. This colorless, hygroscopic, and flammable tertiary amine has a strong 'fishy' odor in low concentrations and an ammonia-like odor at higher concentrations. It is a gas at room temperature but is usually sold in pressurized gas cylinders or as a 40% solution in water.
Monomer	A monomer, pronounced mon'?-m?r, or MON-uh-mer, is a molecule that may bind chemically to other molecules to form a polymer. The term 'monomeric protein' may also be used to describe one of the proteins making up a multiprotein complex. The most common natural monomer is glucose, which is linked by glycosidic bonds into polymers such as cellulose and starch, and is over 77% of the mass of all plant matter.
Polyethylene	Polyethylene or polythene (IUPAC name polyethene or poly(methylene)) is the most common plastic. The annual production is approximately 80 million tonnes. Its primary use is in packaging (plastic bag, plastic films, geomembranes, containers including bottles, etc)..
Polymer	A polymer is a large molecule composed of many repeated subunits, known as monomers. Because of their broad range of properties, both synthetic and natural polymers play an essential and ubiquitous role in everyday life.

17. Radioactivity and Nuclear Chemistry 61018 Organic Chemistry

CHAPTER HIGHLIGHTS & NOTES: KEY TERMS, PEOPLE, PLACES, CONCEPTS

Adipic acid	Adipic acid is the organic compound with the formula $(CH_2)_4(COOH)_2$. From an industrial perspective, it is the most important dicarboxylic acid: About 2.5 billion kilograms of this white crystalline powder are produced annually, mainly as a precursor for the production of nylon. Adipic acid otherwise rarely occurs in nature.
Condensation polymer	Condensation polymers are any kind of polymers formed through a condensation reaction--where molecules join together--losing small molecules as by-products such as water or methanol, as opposed to addition polymers which involve the reaction of unsaturated monomers. Types of condensation polymers include polyamides, polyacetals and polyesters. Condensation polymerization, a form of step-growth polymerization, is a process by which two molecules join together, resulting loss of small molecules which is often water.
Copolymer	A heteropolymer or copolymer is a polymer derived from two monomeric species, as opposed to a homopolymer where only one monomer is used. Copolymerization refers to methods used to chemically synthesize a copolymer. Commercially relevant copolymers include ABS plastic, SBR, Nitrile rubber, styrene-acrylonitrile, styrene-isoprene-styrene (SIS) and ethylene-vinyl acetate.
Hexamethylenediamine	Hexamethylenediamine is the organic compound with the formula $H_2N_6NH_2$. The molecule is a diamine, consisting of a hexamethylene hydrocarbon chain terminated with amine functional groups. The colorless solid (yellowish for some commercial samples) has a strong amine odor, similar to piperidine.
Dimer	A dimer is a chemical entity consisting of two structurally similar monomers joined by bonds that can be either strong or weak, covalent or intermolecular. The term homodimer is used when the two molecules are identical (e.g. A-A) and heterodimer when they are not (e.g. A-B). The reverse of dimerisation is often called dissociation.
Kevlar	Kevlar is the registered trademark for a para-aramid synthetic fiber, related to other aramids such as Nomex and Technora. Developed at DuPont in 1965, this high strength material was first commercially used in the early 1970s as a replacement for steel in racing tires. Typically it is spun into ropes or fabric sheets that can be used as such or as an ingredient in composite material components.

CHAPTER QUIZ: KEY TERMS, PEOPLE, PLACES, CONCEPTS

1. _________ is the chemical compound with the formula C_2H_2. It is a hydrocarbon and the simplest alkyne. This colorless gas is widely used as a fuel and a chemical building block.

a. Gas exchange
b. Bisulfide
c. Buffer solution
d. Acetylene

2. _________ is also known as single displacement reaction and single replacement reaction. In a _________, a functional group in a particular chemical compound is replaced by another group. In organic chemistry, the electrophilic and nucleophilic _________s are of prime importance.

a. Substitution reaction
b. Carbonylation
c. Carbothermic reaction
d. Ceramide phosphoethanolamine synthase

3. In organic chemistry, an _________, olefin, or olefine is an unsaturated chemical compound containing at least one carbon-carbon double bond. The simplest acyclic _________s, with only one double bond and no other functional groups, known as mono-enes, form a homologous series of hydrocarbons with the general formula C_nH_{2n}. They have two hydrogen atoms less than the corresponding alkane (with the same number of carbon atoms)

a. Bacillosamine
b. Alkene
c. 1-Deoxynojirimycin
d. Framycetin

4. _________s are organic compounds and functional groups that contain a basic nitrogen atom with a lone pair. _________s are derivatives of ammonia, wherein one or more hydrogen atoms have been replaced by a substituent such as an alkyl or aryl group. Important _________s include amino acids, biogenic _________s, trimethyl_________, and aniline; see Category:_________s for a list of _________s.

a. Bisulfide
b. Buffering agent
c. Carbonate alkalinity
d. Amine

5. . _________, also known as acetylsalicylic acid (INN (?--?l--i--ik) ASA), is a salicylate drug, often used as an analgesic to relieve minor aches and pains, as an antipyretic to reduce fever, and as an anti-inflammatory medication. _________ was first isolated by Felix Hoffmann, a chemist with the German company Bayer in 1897.

Salicylic acid, the main metabolite of _________, is an integral part of human and animal metabolism.

a. Benzoic acid
b. P-Anisic acid
c. Aspirin
d. 2-Pyridone

ANSWER KEY

17. Radioactivity and Nuclear Chemistry 61018 Organic Chemistry

---

1. d
2. a
3. b
4. d
5. c

---

18. Biochemistry

CHAPTER OUTLINE: KEY TERMS, PEOPLE, PLACES, CONCEPTS

- Aldehyde
- Carbohydrate
- Ketone
- Component
- Monosaccharide
- Digestion
- Disaccharide
- Hexose
- Amylopectin
- Cellulose
- Glycogen
- Polymer
- Polysaccharide
- Simple Sugars
- Fatty acid
- Lipid
- Myristic acid
- Oleic acid
- Polyunsaturated fatty acid
- Stearic acid
- Triglyceride

18. Biochemistry

CHAPTER OUTLINE: KEY TERMS, PEOPLE, PLACES, CONCEPTS

Saturated fat

Unsaturated fat

Phospholipid

Glycolipid

Steroid

Cholesterol

Lipid bilayer

Phosphatidylcholine

Concentration

Amino acid

Enzyme

Side chain

Alanine

Aspartic acid

Lysine

Serine

Dipeptide

Lewis structure

Peptide

Insulin

Hemoglobin

18. Biochemistry

CHAPTER OUTLINE: KEY TERMS, PEOPLE, PLACES, CONCEPTS

- Random coil
- Collagen
- Nucleic acid
- Nucleotide
- Adenine
- Cytosine
- Guanine
- Threonine
- Thymine
- Uracil
- Replication
- Messenger RNA
- Ribosome

18. Biochemistry

CHAPTER HIGHLIGHTS & NOTES: KEY TERMS, PEOPLE, PLACES, CONCEPTS

Aldehyde

An aldehyde is an organic compound containing a formyl group. This functional group, with the structure R-CHO, consists of a carbonyl center (a carbon double bonded to oxygen) bonded to hydrogen and an R group, which is any generic alkyl or side chain. The group without R is called the aldehyde group or formyl group.

Carbohydrate

A carbohydrate is a large biological molecule, or macromolecule, consisting only of carbon, hydrogen (H), and oxygen (O), usually with a hydrogen:oxygen atom ratio of 2:1 (as in water); in other words, with the empirical formula $C_m(H_2O)_n$ (where m could be different from n). Some exceptions exist; for example, deoxyribose, a sugar component of DNA, has the empirical formula $C_5H_{10}O_4$. Carbohydrates are technically hydrates of carbon; structurally it is more accurate to view them as polyhydroxy aldehydes and ketones.

Ketone

In chemistry, a ketone is an organic compound with the structure RC(=O)R', where R and R' can be a variety of carbon-containing substituents. Ketones feature a carbonyl group (C=O) bonded to two other carbon atoms. Many ketones are known and many are of great importance in industry and in biology.

Component

In thermodynamics, a component is a chemically-independent constituent of a system. The number of components represents the minimum number of independent species necessary to define the composition of all phases of the system.

Calculating the number of components in a system is necessary, for example, when applying Gibbs' phase rule in determination of the number of degrees of freedom of a system.

Monosaccharide

Monosaccharides are the most basic units of carbohydrates. They are the simplest form of sugar and are usually colorless, water-soluble, crystalline solids. Some monosaccharides have a sweet taste.

Digestion

In alchemy, digestion is a process in which gentle heat is applied to a substance over a period of several weeks.

This was traditionally performed by sealing a sample of the substance in a flask, and keeping the flask in fresh horse dung or sometimes in direct sunlight. Today, practitioners of alchemy use thermostat-controlled incubators.

Disaccharide

A disaccharide or biose is the carbohydrate formed when two monosaccharides undergo a condensation reaction which involves the elimination of a small molecule, such as water, from the functional groups only. Like monosaccharides, disaccharides form an aqueous solution when dissolved in water. Three common examples are sucrose, lactose, and maltose.

Hexose

In organic chemistry, a hexose is a monosaccharide with six carbon atoms, having the chemical formula $C_6H_{12}O_6$.

Amylopectin	Amylopectin is a soluble polysaccharide and highly branched polymer of glucose found in plants. It is one of the two components of starch, the other being amylose. Glucose units are linked in a linear way with a(1?4) glycosidic bonds.
Cellulose	Cellulose is an organic compound with the formula n, a polysaccharide consisting of a linear chain of several hundred to over ten thousand ß(1?4) linked -glucose units. Cellulose is an important structural component of the primary cell wall of green plants, many forms of algae and the oomycetes. Some species of bacteria secrete it to form biofilms.
Glycogen	Glycogen is a multibranched polysaccharide of glucose that serves as a form of energy storage in animals and fungi. The polysaccharide structure represents the main storage form of glucose in the body. In humans, glycogen is made and stored primarily in the cells of the liver and the muscles, and functions as the secondary long-term energy storage (with the primary energy stores being fats held in adipose tissue).
Polymer	A polymer is a large molecule composed of many repeated subunits, known as monomers. Because of their broad range of properties, both synthetic and natural polymers play an essential and ubiquitous role in everyday life. Polymers range from familiar synthetic plastics such as polystyrene (or styrofoam) to natural biopolymers such as DNA and proteins that are fundamental to biological structure and function.
Polysaccharide	Polysaccharides are polymeric carbohydrate molecules composed of long chains of monosaccharide units bound together by glycosidic bonds. They range in structure from linear to highly branched. Examples include storage polysaccharides such as starch and glycogen, and structural polysaccharides such as cellulose and chitin.
Simple Sugars	Simple Sugars is a Pittsburgh-based cosmetics company run by teen entrepreneur Lani Lazzari. In 2013, Lani Lazzari appeared in Season 4 of the American reality television series Shark Tank where the business received a $100,000 investment from Dallas Mavericks owner Mark Cuban.
Fatty acid	In chemistry, and especially in biochemistry, a fatty acid is a carboxylic acid with a long aliphatic tail, which is either saturated or unsaturated. Most naturally occurring fatty acids have a chain of an even number of carbon atoms, from 4 to 28. Fatty acids are usually derived from triglycerides or phospholipids. When they are not attached to other molecules, they are known as 'free' fatty acids.
Lipid	Lipids are a group of naturally occurring molecules that include fats, waxes, sterols, fat-soluble vitamins, monoglycerides, diglycerides, triglycerides, phospholipids, and others. The main biological functions of lipids include storing energy, signaling, and acting as structural components of cell membranes.

18. Biochemistry

CHAPTER HIGHLIGHTS & NOTES: KEY TERMS, PEOPLE, PLACES, CONCEPTS

Myristic acid	Myristic acid, also called tetradecanoic acid, is a common saturated fatty acid with the molecular formula CH312COOH. A myristate is a salt or ester of myristic acid. Myristic acid is named after the nutmeg Myristica fragrans. Nutmeg butter is 75% trimyristin, the triglyceride of myristic acid.
Oleic acid	Oleic acid is a fatty acid that occurs naturally in various animal and vegetable fats and oils. It is an odorless, colourless oil, although commercial samples may be yellowish. In chemical terms, oleic acid is classified as a monounsaturated omega-9 fatty acid, abbreviated with a lipid number of 18:1 cis-9. It has the formula $CH_3(CH_2)_7CH=CH(CH_2)_7COOH$. The term 'oleic' means related to, or derived from, oil or olive, the oil that is predominantly composed of oleic acid.
Polyunsaturated fatty acid	Polyunsaturated fatty acids are fatty acids that contain more than one double bond in their backbone. This class includes many important compounds, such as essential fatty acids and those that give drying oils their characteristic property. Polyunsaturated fatty acids can be classified in various groups by their chemical structure:
Stearic acid	Stearic acid is the saturated fatty acid with an 18-carbon chain and has the IUPAC name octadecanoic acid. It is a waxy solid, and its chemical formula is $CH_3(CH_2)_{16}CO_2H$. Its name comes from the Greek word st?a? 'stéar', which means tallow. The salts and esters of stearic acid are called stearates.
Triglyceride	A triglyceride is an ester derived from glycerol and three fatty acids. Triglycerides are a blood lipid that help enable the bidirectional transference of adipose fat and blood glucose from the liver. There are many triglycerides: depending on the oil source, some are highly unsaturated, some less so.
Saturated fat	Saturated fat is fat that consists of triglycerides containing only saturated fatty acids. Saturated fatty acids have no double bonds between the individual carbon atoms of the fatty acid chain. That is, the chain of carbon atoms is fully 'saturated' with hydrogen atoms.
Unsaturated fat	An unsaturated fat is a fat or fatty acid in which there is at least one double bond within the fatty acid chain. A fatty acid chain is monounsaturated if it contains one double bond, and polyunsaturated if it contains more than one double bond. Where double bonds are formed, hydrogen atoms are eliminated.
Phospholipid	Phospholipids are a class of lipids that are a major component of all cell membranes as they can form lipid bilayers. Most phospholipids contain a diglyceride, a phosphate group, and a simple organic molecule such as choline; one exception to this rule is sphingomyelin, which is derived from sphingosine instead of glycerol.

The first phospholipid identified as such in biological tissues was lecithin, or phosphatidylcholine, in the egg yolk, by Theodore Nicolas Gobley, a French chemist and pharmacist, in 1847. The structure of the phospholipid molecule generally consists of hydrophobic tails and a hydrophilic head.

Glycolipid

Glycolipids are lipids with a carbohydrate attached. Their role is to provide energy and also serve as markers for cellular recognition.

Steroid

A steroid is a type of organic compound that contains a characteristic arrangement of four cycloalkane rings that are joined to each other. Examples of steroids include the dietary fat cholesterol, the sex hormones estradiol and testosterone and the anti-inflammatory drug dexamethasone.

The core of steroids is composed of twenty carbon atoms bonded together that take the form of four fused rings: three cyclohexane rings (designated as rings A, B and C in the figure to the right) and one cyclopentane ring (the D ring).

Cholesterol

Cholesterol, from the Ancient Greek chole- and stereos (solid) followed by the chemical suffix -ol for an alcohol, is an organic molecule. It is a sterol (or modified steroid), and an essential structural component of animal cell membranes that is required to establish proper membrane permeability and fluidity. Cholesterol is thus considered within the class of lipid molecules.

Lipid bilayer

The lipid bilayer is a thin polar membrane made of two layers of lipid molecules. These membranes are flat sheets that form a continuous barrier around cells. The cell membrane of almost all living organisms and many viruses are made of a lipid bilayer, as are the membranes surrounding the cell nucleus and other sub-cellular structures.

Phosphatidylcholine

Phosphatidylcholines are a class of phospholipids that incorporate choline as a headgroup. They are a major component of biological membranes and can be easily obtained from a variety of readily available sources, such as egg yolk or soybeans, from which they are mechanically or chemically extracted using hexane. They are also a member of the lecithin group of yellow-brownish fatty substances occurring in animal and plant tissues.

Concentration

In chemistry, concentration is the abundance of a constituent divided by the total volume of a mixture. Several types of mathematical description can be distinguished: mass concentration, molar concentration, number concentration, and volume concentration. The term concentration can be applied to any kind of chemical mixture, but most frequently it refers to solutes and solvents in solutions.

Amino acid

Amino acids are biologically important organic compounds made from amine ($-NH_2$) and carboxylic acid ($-COOH$) functional groups, along with a side-chain specific to each amino acid.

18. Biochemistry

CHAPTER HIGHLIGHTS & NOTES: KEY TERMS, PEOPLE, PLACES, CONCEPTS

The key elements of an amino acid are carbon, hydrogen, oxygen, and nitrogen, though other elements are found in the side-chains of certain amino acids. About 500 amino acids are known and can be classified in many ways.

Enzyme

Enzymes are large biological molecules responsible for the thousands of metabolic processes that sustain life. They are highly selective catalysts, greatly accelerating both the rate and specificity of metabolic reactions, from the digestion of food to the synthesis of DNA. Most enzymes are proteins, although some catalytic RNA molecules have been identified. Enzymes adopt a specific three-dimensional structure, and may employ organic (e.g. biotin) and inorganic (e.g. magnesium ion) cofactors to assist in catalysis.

Side chain

In organic chemistry and biochemistry, a side chain is a chemical group that is attached to a core part of the molecule called 'main chain' or backbone. The placeholder R is often used as a generic placeholder for alkyl (saturated hydrocarbon) group side chains in chemical structure diagrams. To indicate other non-carbon groups in structure diagrams, X, Y, or Z is often used.

Alanine

Alanine is an a-amino acid with the chemical formula $CH_3CH(NH_2)COOH$. The -isomer is one of the 20 amino acids encoded by the genetic code. Its codons are GCU, GCC, GCA, and GCG. It is classified as a nonpolar amino acid. -Alanine is second only to leucine in rate of occurrence, accounting for 7.8% of the primary structure in a sample of 1,150 proteins.

Aspartic acid

Aspartic acid is an a-amino acid with the chemical formula $HOOCCH(NH_2)CH_2COOH$. The carboxylate anion, salt, or ester of aspartic acid is known as aspartate. The -isomer of aspartate is one of the 22 proteinogenic amino acids, i.e., the building blocks of proteins. Its codons are GAU and GAC.

Aspartic acid is, together with glutamic acid, classified as an acidic amino acid with a pK_a of 3.9, however in a peptide the pK_a is highly dependent on the local environment.

Lysine

Lysine is an a-amino acid with the chemical formula $HO_2CCH(NH_2)(CH_2)_4NH_2$. It is an essential amino acid for humans. Lysine's codons are AAA and AAG.

Lysine is a base, as are arginine and histidine.

Serine

Serine is an amino acid with the formula $HO_2CCH(NH_2)CH_2OH$. It is one of the proteinogenic amino acids. Its codons in the genetic code are UCU, UCC, UCA, UCG, AGU and AGC. By virtue of the hydroxyl group, serine is classified as a polar amino acid.

Dipeptide

A dipeptide is a sometimes ambiguous designation of two classes of organic compounds: Its molecules contain either two amino acids joined by a single peptide bond or one amino acid with two peptide bonds.

Lewis structure	Lewis structures are diagrams that show the bonding between atoms of a molecule and the lone pairs of electrons that may exist in the molecule. A Lewis structure can be drawn for any covalently bonded molecule, as well as coordination compounds. The Lewis structure was named after Gilbert N
Peptide	Peptides are short chains of amino acid monomers linked by peptide bonds. The covalent chemical bonds are formed when the carboxyl group of one amino acid reacts with the amino group of another. The shortest peptides are dipeptides, consisting of 2 amino acids joined by a single peptide bond, followed by tripeptides, tetrapeptides, etc.
Insulin	Insulin is a peptide hormone, produced by beta cells of the pancreas, and is central to regulating carbohydrate and fat metabolism in the body. Insulin causes cells in the liver, skeletal muscles, and fat tissue to absorb glucose from the blood. In the liver and skeletal muscles, glucose is stored as glycogen, and in fat cells (adipocytes) it is stored as triglycerides.
Hemoglobin	Hemoglobin; also spelled haemoglobin and abbreviated Hb or Hgb, is the iron-containing oxygen-transport metalloprotein in the red blood cells of all vertebrates as well as the tissues of some invertebrates. Hemoglobin in the blood carries oxygen from the respiratory organs (lungs or gills) to the rest of the body (i.e. the tissues) where it releases the oxygen to burn nutrients to provide energy to power the functions of the organism, and collects the resultant carbon dioxide to bring it back to the respiratory organs to be dispensed from the organism. In mammals, the protein makes up about 97% of the red blood cells' dry content (by weight), and around 35% of the total content (including water).
Random coil	A random coil is a polymer conformation where the monomer subunits are oriented randomly while still being bonded to adjacent units. It is not one specific shape, but a statistical distribution of shapes for all the chains in a population of macromolecules. The conformation's name is derived from the idea that, in the absence of specific, stabilizing interactions, a polymer backbone will 'sample' all possible conformations randomly.
Collagen	Collagen is the main structural protein of the various connective tissues in animals. (The name collagen comes from the Greek kolla meaning glue and suffix -gen denoting producing). As the main component of connective tissue, it is the most abundant protein in mammals, making up from 25% to 35% of the whole-body protein content.
Nucleic acid	Nucleic acids are polymeric macromolecules, or large biological molecules, essential for all known forms of life. Nucleic acids, which include DNA (deoxyribonucleic acid) and RNA (ribonucleic acid), are made from monomers known as nucleotides. Each nucleotide has three components: a 5-carbon sugar, a phosphate group, and a nitrogenous base.

18. Biochemistry

CHAPTER HIGHLIGHTS & NOTES: KEY TERMS, PEOPLE, PLACES, CONCEPTS

Nucleotide	Nucleotides are organic molecules that serve as the monomers, or subunits, of nucleic acids like DNA and RNA. The building blocks of nucleic acids, nucleotides are composed of a nitrogenous base, a five-carbon sugar (ribose or deoxyribose), and at least one phosphate group. Nucleotides serve to carry packets of energy within the cell (ATP). In the form of the nucleoside triphosphates (ATP, GTP, CTP and UTP), nucleotides play central roles in metabolism.
Adenine	Adenine is a nucleobase (a purine derivative) with a variety of roles in biochemistry including cellular respiration, in the form of both the energy-rich adenosine triphosphate (ATP) and the cofactors nicotinamide adenine dinucleotide (NAD) and flavin adenine dinucleotide (FAD), and protein synthesis, as a chemical component of DNA and RNA. The shape of adenine is complementary to either thymine in DNA or uracil in RNA.
Cytosine	Cytosine is one of the four main bases found in DNA and RNA, along with adenine, guanine, and thymine (uracil in RNA). It is a pyrimidine derivative, with a heterocyclic aromatic ring and two substituents attached (an amine group at position 4 and a keto group at position 2). The nucleoside of cytosine is cytidine.
Guanine	Guanine is one of the four main nucleobases found in the nucleic acids DNA and RNA, the others being adenine, cytosine, and thymine (uracil in RNA). In DNA, guanine is paired with cytosine. With the formula $C_5H_5N_5O$, guanine is a derivative of purine, consisting of a fused pyrimidine-imidazole ring system with conjugated double bonds.
Threonine	Threonine is an a-amino acid with the chemical formula $HO_2CCH(NH_2)CH(OH)CH_3$. Its codons are ACU, ACA, ACC, and ACG. This essential amino acid is classified as polar. Together with serine, threonine is one of two proteinogenic amino acids bearing an alcohol group (tyrosine is not an alcohol but a phenol, since its hydroxyl group is bonded directly to an aromatic ring, giving it different acid/base and oxidative properties).
Thymine	Thymine is one of the four nucleobases in the nucleic acid of DNA that are represented by the letters G-C-A-T. The others are adenine, guanine, and cytosine. Thymine is also known as 5-methyluracil, a pyrimidine nucleobase.
Uracil	Uracil is one of the four nucleobases in the nucleic acid of RNA that are represented by the letters A, G, C and U. The others are adenine (A), cytosine, and guanine. In RNA, uracil binds to adenine via two hydrogen bonds. In DNA, the uracil nucleobase is replaced by thymine.
Replication	Replication, in metallography, is the use of thin plastic films to nondestructively duplicate the microstructure of a component. The film is then examined at high magnifications.

CHAPTER HIGHLIGHTS & NOTES: KEY TERMS, PEOPLE, PLACES, CONCEPTS

Messenger RNA	Messenger RNA is a large family of RNA molecules that convey genetic information from DNA to the ribosome, where they specify the amino acid sequence of the protein products of gene expression. Following transcription of mRNA by RNA polymerase, the mRNA is translated into a polymer of amino acids: a protein, as summarized in the central dogma of molecular biology. As in DNA, mRNA genetic information is encoded in the sequence of nucleotides, which are arranged into codons consisting of three bases each.
Ribosome	The ribosome is a large and complex molecular machine, found within all living cells, that serves as the primary site of biological protein synthesis (translation). Ribosomes link amino acids together in the order specified by messenger RNA (mRNA) molecules. Ribosomes consist of two major subunits--the small ribosomal subunit reads the mRNA, while the large subunit joins amino acids to form a polypeptide chain.

CHAPTER QUIZ: KEY TERMS, PEOPLE, PLACES, CONCEPTS

1. _________s are lipids with a carbohydrate attached. Their role is to provide energy and also serve as markers for cellular recognition.

   a. Carbohydrate acetalisation
   b. Carbohydrate chemistry
   c. Glycolipid
   d. Chemical glycosylation

2. _________ is a soluble polysaccharide and highly branched polymer of glucose found in plants. It is one of the two components of starch, the other being amylose.

   Glucose units are linked in a linear way with a(1?4) glycosidic bonds.

   a. Amylopectin
   b. Carbohydrate conformation
   c. Carbohydrate chemistry
   d. Carbohydrate acetalisation

3. . An _________ is an organic compound containing a formyl group. This functional group, with the structure R-CHO, consists of a carbonyl center (a carbon double bonded to oxygen) bonded to hydrogen and an R group, which is any generic alkyl or side chain. The group without R is called the _________ group or formyl group.

   a. Bacillosamine

b. Chitobiose
c. 1-Deoxynojirimycin
d. Aldehyde

4. _________ is an a-amino acid with the chemical formula $HO_2CCH(NH_2)(CH_2)_4NH_2$. It is an essential amino acid for humans. _________'s codons are AAA and AAG.

   _________ is a base, as are arginine and histidine.

   a. Lysine
   b. 2,6-Dihydroxypyridine
   c. 2-Pyridone
   d. Ciclopirox

5. A _________ is a large biological molecule, or macromolecule, consisting only of carbon, hydrogen (H), and oxygen (O), usually with a hydrogen:oxygen atom ratio of 2:1 (as in water); in other words, with the empirical formula $C_m(H_2O)_n$ (where m could be different from n). Some exceptions exist; for example, deoxyribose, a sugar component of DNA, has the empirical formula $C_5H_{10}O_4$. _________s are technically hydrates of carbon; structurally it is more accurate to view them as polyhydroxy aldehydes and ketones.

   a. Biodiesel production
   b. Carbohydrate conformation
   c. Carbohydrate chemistry
   d. Carbohydrate

ANSWER KEY
18. Biochemistry

1. c
2. a
3. d
4. a
5. d

CPSIA information can be obtained
at www.ICGtesting.com
Printed in the USA
FSHW012033130819
61029FS

9 781497 005228